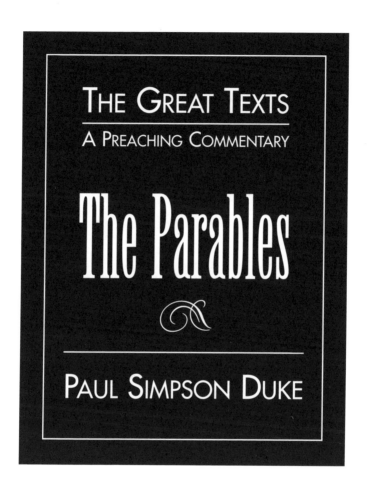

THE GREAT TEXTS

A PREACHING COMMENTARY

The Parables

PAUL SIMPSON DUKE

Abingdon Press
Nashville

THE PARABLES
A PREACHING COMMENTARY

Library of Congress Cataloging-in-Publication Data

Duke, Paul Simpson.
   The parables : a preaching commentary / Paul Simpson Duke.
      p. cm.
   Includes bibliographical references (p.   ).
   ISBN 0-687-09049-0 (binding: pbk. : alk. paper)
1. Jesus Christ—Parables—Homiletical use.   I. Title.

   BT375.3.D85 2005
   226.8'06—dc22

                                                                                      2005004131

05 06 07 08 09 10 11 12 13 14—10 9 8 7 6 5 4 3 2 1

MANUFACTURED IN THE UNITED STATES OF AMERICA

for Stephanie Duke Ezell

and Christopher Chandler Duke,

parables for me of grace

Contents

Acknowledgments

My work on this book was nurtured and sustained by the kindness of good partners and friends. I owe a great debt of thanks to John Holbert, the editor of this series, who invited me to write and gave good guidance for the work, and more, extended extraordinary grace and encouragement to me along the way. Bob Ratcliff, editor at Abingdon Press, has also been the soul of generous friendship and forbearance. My gratitude to these two men runs very deep.

An earlier version of chapter 1 was delivered as the Purcell Bible Conference Lecture at Barton College in 2000. The hospitality and care given to me by the religion department there on more than one occasion are a warm and grateful recollection.

The First Baptist Church of Ann Arbor, Michigan, which my wife and I are privileged to serve, is a beautifully generous community of support. Among the congregation's many good gifts to their pastors is annual study leave, much of which lately for me was devoted to this project. I am enduringly thankful to them.

My greatest and happiest debt of thanks is to my wife, Stacey Simpson Duke. Her love and support in all things are miraculous to me. Much work on this book was done during her pregnancy with our twin sons, Rob and Charlie, and during their first weeks of life. When her own load was heaviest and her hands were more than full, she not only blessed me with time to write, but she pitched in to help, reading these pages with a keen eye for needed corrections and giving wondrous encouragement. I sing her praise.

CHAPTER ONE

Into the World of the Parables

Imagine the Scriptures as a house, a mansion of huge proportions. Suppose we are taking a tour of this house. We are led through many large rooms, like galleries. Each gallery turns out to be a kind of theater in which actors perform different types of scripture. Every room features one biblical *form* in multiple performances. In one room the great primal narratives are performed. In other rooms different kinds of psalms are sung. In still others are prophets chanting oracles, sages pronouncing proverbs, apostles reading their correspondence to the churches. Several galleries feature stories from the Gospels. In different rooms are performances of Jesus' birth, his miracles, his pronouncements, his passion, his resurrection appearances. But there is one room that stands out as uniquely curious, beguiling, and strange—the gallery of his parables.

Inhabiting this room is an odd assortment of colorful characters: we see a sneaky financial officer being praised by the boss who just fired him, a farmer shrugging off an invasion of weeds, a gardener fertilizing a dead tree, an extortionist saying his prayers, a half-breed paying the bills of a battered man who hates his kind. There is a woman shouting at a judge, another peering under furniture, and another who gives us a wink while hiding a pinch of yeast in a huge batch of dough. This gallery is crowded with mad farmers, rascals, beggars, slaves, and kings. It performs business deals, harvests, huge parties, extravagant pardons, and riveting punishments.

What a strange world we have entered here. Within the house of biblical forms, Jesus' parables are unique. Here we find a body of deliberate fictions peopled with characters whose behavior is often irregular, if not absurd. The plots take astonishing turns. There is a wildness in these tales, a recurring capacity to shock. The parables are difficult to pin down. We may decide what one of them "means," but a closer look discloses other possible meanings— while yet further reflection reveals something larger and more elusive, less like a *meaning* and more like a reverberating *encounter*. Such encounters may leave us scratching our heads.

For these reasons and more, the parables pose a special challenge to those of us who preach. They are very rich, very inviting; they bear powerfully and often beautifully the very core of the gospel. They are also, as a rule, highly complex and resistant to easy explanation. Tom Long puts it nicely: "Preaching on a parable is a novice preacher's dream but often an experienced preacher's nightmare."[1] We will explore how we may enter the parables with keener sensitivity to what they do, and how we might preach them in ways that honor them and continue their amazing work.

A Preliminary Amazement

Before we take the first step in studying the parables, it would be worthwhile to pause and let ourselves be amazed. The stories Jesus told are like old friends to us now, so naturally we forget to be surprised by their existence. This is a little like walking through your house not noticing that the walls are hung with dozens of original Rembrandts, van Goghs, and O'Keeffes.

Think of it this way. Would we really have expected Jesus, on top of everything else he did and was, to be such a teller of tales? The church calls him the Christ, Lord, Savior, the Word made flesh. Suppose we were looking for such a person in the world; what would we expect? We would expect someone beautifully good, showing tenderness to the sick, gentleness to children, and a proper rage against oppression. We might expect withering words against hypocrisy and mercy for sinners. We might well expect mighty works and wonders. It would not surprise us to find vast sorrow in his eyes and a wild joy. If we were uncommonly discerning, we might even expect that such a life would finally heave the sins of the world on its shoulders into a terrible death. But what could have led us to expect that he would be a narrative artist, a spinner of brilliant fictions? Many who hold no faith in Jesus recognize in him a narrative genius.

On the whole, the church has not. We value his parables but are unsurprised by them. Perhaps the assumption is as follows: *of course* he told stories! Loving as he did the common folk, Jesus would naturally be generous with earthy analogies from everyday life, accessible stories to help the people see what he meant. A teacher with his kind of heart would fill his talk with luminous illustrations for his hearers.

Such a view of the parables is dangerously naive and guarantees failure to hear them. There *is*, in fact, something about the parables that can rightly be called central, essential, even necessary, to the message and the life of Jesus; but this is precisely because they are not simple illustrations. Like him, they come to us as mysteries, as depth, as encounter. Like him, they are subversive and dangerous. Like him, they signify more than can be said. They do more than point to the reign of God; they are something like narrative incarnations of it. And they are amazing.

But we are already ahead of ourselves. Having ventured that a proper beginning with the parables is to notice that they are wondrous, we now turn to the business of asking what a parable is and what a parable does.

THE PARAMETERS OF PARABLE

The available literature on Jesus' parables is immense, even daunting. Recent parable study has been explosively profuse and diverse. The parameters of this book do not permit a complete survey of that literature or any full discussion of the many ways that parables have been understood. But a brief exploration into the essential character of parables is in order. Perhaps the best way to begin is this: the parables of Jesus are a specialized subset of a broader range of Jewish figurative speech.

The Hebrew word for the full range of figurative speech is *mashal*, the root of which means "to be like." *Mashal* is used for all kinds of figurative or allusive expression, including proverbs, riddles, stories, allegories, and analogies. Even a person can be called a *mashal*. Job uses the word when he cries that God has made him "a byword" (Job 17:6; cf. Ps 44:14).

When the Hebrew Scriptures and other writings were translated into Greek for what we know as the Septuagint, the word *mashal*, in most instances, was rendered *parabolē*, an apt word for figurative speech since it refers literally to something "thrown beside." This Greek word retained a broad range of applications, as is clear from the way that the Gospel writers employed it. For example, when Mark and Matthew report Jesus' comparison of a fig tree's leaves to signs of the end time, it is called a *parabolē*, (Mark 13:28; Matt 24:32; NRSV translates, "lesson"). When Jesus declares that a person is defiled not by what goes in but by what comes out, the disciples call it a *parabolē*, (Mark 7:17; Matt 15:15). Luke employs *parabolē*, for several proverbs, including the one about the blind leading the blind (6:39; cf. 4:32; 5:36; 12:41).

Clearly then, the sense of the word *parable* in the Synoptic Gospels (John's Gospel neither uses the word nor reports any stories told by Jesus) is by no means limited to the stories that we call his parables. The tales he told were part of a larger traditional way of speech that was figurative or allusive and often metaphorical.

The fact remains that the stories themselves stand out as a unique form within the body of Jesus' speech. As fictions featuring characters and plot, they constitute a quite distinctive mode of his proclamation; they bear unusual powers of disclosure, and they present special challenges to the preacher. We have good reason to consider them as a separate form and to call them, uniquely, his parables.

This doesn't mean that they are all full-blown narratives. Some parables have only the rudiments of plot. Consider, for example, the comparison of the kingdom of God to a woman who hides yeast in a large amount of dough (Matt 13:33; Luke 13:20-21). Its form is not a straightforward story (e.g., "A certain woman took some yeast") but a comparison ("It is like yeast that a woman took"); yet we are still given the sketch of a plot: the woman takes it and hides it, then in time the whole batch is leavened. The presence of such rudimentary plots in several of the comparisons made by Jesus permits us to count them among his parables.

A JEWISH MUSIC

Jesus' parables are entirely and marvelously Jewish. They sprang from a Jewish mind that drew broadly and deeply from his people's traditions, images, characters, plots, and themes. In this regard, there has been some question as to how original or unique his parables were. The issue bears at least a brief consideration here.

Varying claims are made about the relationship between the parables of Jesus and the rabbinic parables in the later Talmud and Midrash. Perhaps too much has been claimed on both sides of the question. One striking fact is reported by Bernard Scott, citing the work of Jacob Neusner: "A survey of the rabbinic materials turns up a curious anomaly. In those layers of tradition that can be isolated as belonging to the Pharisees, there are no parables."[2] It must be stressed that this apparent silence does not mean that Jesus was alone in telling parables in his day. It is not impossible that some of the Talmudic parables have their origin in the Second Temple period.[3]

We must be cautious, then, in what we claim about the uniqueness of Jesus' parables. Joachim Jeremias surely overstated the case when he declared, "Jesus' parables are something entirely new."[4] What can be said is this: (1) Jesus' parables are consistent with the figurative repertoire of the Jewish tradition, including some parabolic narratives told by prophets (e.g., 2 Sam 12:1-4; Isa 5:1-7). (2) Whether or not his contemporaries told parables, Jesus was remembered not only for the force of his parables but also for the sheer preponderance of them. Aside from testimony that "without a parable he told them nothing" (Matt 13:34; Mark 4:34), a full third of what we have as the sayings of Jesus is made up of parables. (3) His parables have unique qualities of genius, beauty, stunning complexities, and evocative power. George Buttrick said it this way: "Jesus did not invent this form of story, but under His transforming touch its water became wine. The sonata existed before Beethoven."[5]

Central to understanding the parables of Jesus as quintessentially Jewish is their character as highly imaginative theological speech. David Stern says of the parables of the rabbis, "Above all else, the *mashal* represents the greatest effort to imagine God in all rabbinic literature."[6] The fictions of Jesus offer radical imaginings of God, inviting their hearers to nothing less than the re-imagining of reality itself.[7]

Imaginative evocations of God were integral to the task of Israel's poets, prophets, and sages. Yahweh—who can never be carved or kept or used, whose ways are a sovereign, insistent wildness—is served by a constant renewal of imagination. To become and remain the people of such a God among the persuasive structures of idolatry in the world requires revolutionary re-imagining of God's reign among us. The parables of Jesus, in continuity with the speech of Israel's other prophets and teachers, are acts of imagination to awaken imaginative responses toward the living God.

THE PARABLES' FREEDOM

The history of parable interpretation is crowded with claims about what they must and must not mean. Perhaps it is inevitable that such imaginative tales should prompt managerial responses. From the earliest days of the church until the late nineteenth century, the predominant hermeneutical device with parables was to discover secret, often elaborate, allegorical meanings. The impetus for reading the parables allegorically was derived from the Gospels themselves, which append such readings to some parables.

In 1888 Adolf Jülicher brilliantly demolished the allegorical hermeneutic, but he replaced one excess with another. All parables, he claimed, can be reduced to a single point of meaning. His critical insights notwithstanding, the single points discovered by Jülicher turned out to be identical with the slogans of nineteenth-century liberalism.

The works of C. H. Dodd[8] and Jeremias in the mid-twentieth century built on Jülicher's work while critiquing his interpretations. For them, the locus of all the parables was eschatological—the kingdom of God. Their meanings, especially for Jeremias, must be found in the life-situations of Jesus' ministry. Dan Via countered that as aesthetic literary objects, the parables possess their own independent and existential force, whatever their originating contexts may have been.[9] Many literary-critical studies followed, focused on the parables' essential character as metaphor or symbol.[10] But increasingly this approach has been coupled with strong interest in reconstructing the intentions of the historical Jesus and, if not his original words, the original parameters and plots of his parables[11] and the first-century social realities they reflect and address. Many scholars now read the parables through the lens of social-science theory, often asserting that the original parables were pedagogical commentaries on socioeconomic injustice.[12]

Such diversity of interpretation is in part a tribute to the explosion of critical methods and in part a tribute to the multilayered suggestiveness of the parables themselves. What must be avoided, and often is not, is the making of rigid pronouncements on what a parable of Jesus can and cannot be. For example, by what authority can it really be said that no parable of Jesus could have carried allegorical elements? Such a claim is arbitrary and assumes Jesus was above using a narrative device found in his own Scriptures. Or again, why limit a parable's application to one kind of circumstance in Jesus' ministry, when it is quite possible that he performed the same parable on different occasions with different nuance?[13] For that matter, when a parable attributed to him is, by our standards, in some theological tension with others of his sayings, who is to say that he cannot have spoken it or something very like it? Through different seasons, in different circumstances, and toward different hearers, his sense of the divine mystery may have required less "consistency" than do we.

Part of what we have called the parables' "freedom" pertains to their character as metaphor or poetic expression. The language of metaphor or poetic images yields not one-dimensional meaning but an expansive suggestiveness or elasticity of meaning. Though parables are not Rorschach tests for undisciplined free association,[14] we can rightly think of a certain polyvalence of meaning in them. They may invite us to more than one trajectory of reflection, more than one possibility for decision. For preachers, this is bad news and good news. The bad news is that choosing how to preach a parable—especially choosing what to leave out—can be a maddening decision. The good news is that there is no single correct way to preach any parable.

It is in the nature of parable to be unpredictable. Like Jesus himself, parables refuse the management of neat categories; they come to us on their own terms. To hear them requires uncommon openness, a suspension of expectation, a lightness on the feet. This is not to say that we dispense with our critical faculties. But since Jesus generally unloosed these stories as instruments of surprise, we would be wise to receive them without having already concluded what they can and cannot do.

Having cautioned ourselves against presupposing too much, we are in a better position to acknowledge certain tendencies, at least, in the parables of Jesus. The remainder of this chapter seeks to describe these patterns in the hope that familiarity with them may sharpen our sensitivities to what the parables intend.

THE ASPECT OF THE EARTHY

The parables are secular stories; they point to the actual world of mundane objects, occurrences, and relationships. In the tales told by Jesus we encounter no talking animals, no giants or heroes or magic or mighty works. Nor do the parables take us to exotic places; they unfold right here at home. Two parables form an exception by reporting afterlife conversations (Matt 25:31-46; Luke 16:19-31), but, strikingly, both do so only to point back to the most common earthy acts. The stock-in-trade of Jesus' parables is always the familiar mundane: crops, a coin, a callous judge, employers and employees, farmers, cooks, travelers between two actual cities, family conflict.

Theologically, this is rich. As Amos Wilder said, "What does this mean except that he brought theology down into daily life and into the immediate everyday situation? Here is a clue for the preacher, indeed for the Christian whatever his [or her] form of witness." Jesus in the parables "shows that for him [our] destiny is at stake in [our] ordinary creaturely existence, domestic, economic and social."[15]

Even so, the fact that the parables have their setting in common life presents us with a problem. The everyday life of Jesus' day is far removed from our own, which means that the effect of the parables can be easily lost on us. To our ears, stories about kings, masters, slaves, Pharisees, toll collectors, and the road from Jerusalem to Jericho have a long-ago-and-far-away feel—almost the feel of fairy tales—and so precisely the opposite effect that they originally had. The first hearers of the parables lived among these figures and places, and also within the customs, values, laws, and economic relationships that underlie the stories. The parables, in other words, took place within the actual landscape of their lives and did their work by means of what we call "the scandal of recognition." Since our lives are lived on foreign landscapes, how can the parables do their full work with us? How can preachers bridge the gap to create the starkly real-life recognition that the parables intend? The answer to that question is complex enough and crucial enough that we will return to it often.

A Profusion of Surprises

From their settings in the ordinary, the parables have a wild way of leaping to the extraordinary. Almost all of them take strange turns, ranging from the quirky to the truly astounding. Clearly, Jesus used parables as strategic instruments of surprise. Consider some examples.

A rich man hears that his chief business officer mismanaged funds. "You're fired," he says. "Turn in the books." The manager goes out talking to himself: "What will I do? I'm too weak to dig and too proud to beg. I know what I'll do; I'll make me some friends." So he tracks down everyone who owes money to his boss and tells the people to pay less than they owe—for which the boss praises him (Luke 16:1-8*a*). Strange.

Or again, a king gives a wedding feast for his son. After some unpleasant business with invited guests who refuse to attend, the king invites people from the streets to join the party, and they fill up his hall. Mingling among the street people, he spots one who isn't in proper dress for a wedding and flies into a rage. "How did you get in?" he says and then throws him into outer darkness (Matt 22:1-14). Very strange.

Sometimes the plot of a parable comes from comparing God's reign with something unclean. The kingdom of heaven is like yeast that a woman took and hid in three measures of flour until all of it was leavened (Matt 13:33; Luke 13:21). To us there is no surprise here. But in Jesus' world, yeast was a symbol of impurity. And the kingdom is like a *woman … hiding … that stuff* in a mountain of dough till all of it is infected? Or again, the kingdom "is like a mustard seed that someone took and sowed in the garden" (Luke 13:18-19; cf. Matt 13:31-32; Mark 4:30-32). But the law forbids planting mustard in the garden. Mustard can be planted only by the edge of the field, separate from the garden; otherwise the whole garden is rendered unclean.[16] Besides, the standard botanical image of God's reign is the great cedar (Ezek 17:22-24), not a weedy shrub.

Most often the element of shock in a parable occurs in a strange course of action taken by a central character. Typically, this action is a kind of absurd extravagance. What kind of shepherd is so obsessed with a single stray that he leaves ninety-nine sheep untended in the wild to look for it (Matt 18:12-13; Luke 15:4-6)? What kind of woman, so poor she turns her house upside down to scrape up a single coin, would throw a party for the neighbors when she found it (Luke 15:8-9)? What farmer, finding his wheat infested with weeds, says, "Let 'em grow!" (Matt 13:24-30)? If a landowner's tenants have murdered the servants he already sent to collect what they owe, what kind of insane risk does he take to send not the cops but his son to their door (Matt 21:33-41; Mark 12:1-9; Luke 20:9-16)? Sensible employers don't pay a day's wage for an hour's work (Matt 20:1-15). A respectable father doesn't throw a party for a son who just blew a third of the estate on a joy ride, or go equally eager to embrace a son who hates his ways (Luke 15:11-32).

Soon, we will consider a particular implication of these oddly behaving central characters. For now, let it suffice to say that they are one manifestation of a consistent pattern in the parables: the factor of surprise. It would be wrong to claim that every parable does its work this way. A man builds his house on sand and it comes crashing down (Matt 7:24-27; Luke 6:48-49)—no surprise there, except that the man is surprisingly dumb! Or again, when Jesus speaks of someone estimating the cost of a tower before starting to build it, or a king calculating his troop strength before going to war (Luke 14:28-32), no shock value is present. But in so many parables is something unexpected or somehow "off" that we would do well—always—to look for it. Since we already know these stories, or think we do, this openness to embedded surprises becomes something of a discipline. Without such discipline—coming to these stories each time as if for the first time—we will reduce the parables to object lessons for our use instead of finding in them the occasions of encounter.

THE FUNCTION OF DISORIENTATION

The element of surprise in a parable can leave listeners in a quandary. We are left to sort out what this strangeness means.

We are pressed into having to decide something about the story, which may also invite us to decide something about ourselves.[17] Many parables do this forcefully by means of a very sudden, unexpected ending—an ending that springs open like a trap-door at our feet and sends us falling, sliding down the curve of a question.

C. H. Dodd gave a definition of *parable* that is classic: "At its simplest, the parable is a metaphor or simile drawn from nature or common life, arresting the hearer by its vividness or strangeness, and leaving the mind in sufficient doubt about its precise application to tease it into active thought."[18] The novelist Ron Hansen puts it this way:

> Parables invite the hearer's interest with familiar settings and situations but finally veer off into the unfamiliar, shattering their homey realism and insisting on further reflection and inquiry. We have the uneasy feeling that *we* are being interpreted even as we interpret them.[19]

The "veering off into the unfamiliar" creates disorientation, "leaving the mind in sufficient doubt" that we must rethink everything, including the possibility that "*we* are being interpreted."

It is as if a parable were a journey on which Jesus is our guide. He takes us through landscapes that we know. We recognize this feature and that, and relax into comfort. Then, abruptly, the scenery turns strange, even surreal. The inhabitants become bizarre. Suddenly, Jesus disappears; the tour is over. Looking around us, we see we have arrived at nothing that looks like a destination; it is more like a crossroads. Where we go from here is a puzzle left for us to discern.

For an altogether different analogy of the disorienting quality of parable, consider the poem "Pitcher" by Robert Francis. The poem describes a baseball pitcher and is apropos of the teller of parables.

> *His art is eccentricity, his aim*
> *How not to hit the mark he seems to aim at,*
>
> *His passion how to avoid the obvious,*
> *His technique how to vary the avoidance.*

The others throw to be comprehended. He
Throws to be a moment misunderstood.

Yet not too much. Not errant, arrant, wild,
But every seeming aberration willed.

Not to, yet still, still to communicate
Making the batter understand too late.[20]

There is often something in Jesus' parables that seems intended to baffle. Like a good pitcher, "He / Throws to be a moment misunderstood. / Yet not too much." He sets up an expectation, then gives us something else. We can't tell what the pitch will be. It seems to head for the center of the plate, then curves wide, beyond our reach. It zooms at our heads—bail out!—then cuts to the plate for a strike. He varies his pitches: fastball, off-speed, inside, outside, knuckleball, curve. We are kept off balance. We can't hit him. But all the while, he is teaching us. It is not purely "content" that he teaches. It is the baffling experience itself he teaches, an experience that communnicates more than we expected (or wanted?) about who God is and who we are. Perhaps he is also teaching us in the parables to listen and live with sharper ears and wider eyes, paying closer attention everywhere, holding freer and wilder expectations.

THE SMALLNESS OF TITLES

If all we have observed about the parables' lively freedom is true, then we should know that the titles we assign to them are generally a bad idea. All the titles of Jesus' parables are our inventions. The habit goes back at least to the third century in a Gnostic tractate called *The Apocryphon of James*. But can you imagine Jesus saying, "Here's a little story I like to call 'The Good Samaritan'"? He didn't announce his pitches.

To face a parable with a title in mind is like watching it through thick tinted glasses. Colors are screened out, movement blurred, nuances unseen. What if we didn't call it "The Good Samaritan" but "The Parable of the Pathetic Priest and the Lousy Levite" or "The Parable of the Wounded Traveler"? Would we see something different, miss something different? The most famously disastrous naming of a parable is, of course, "The Prodigal Son," a title that lops off half the story. But even to call it "The Prodigal Father," as some have done, is to assume a certain position toward the story before we hear it. It is best to face the parables, insofar as possible, without position and without the protective, limiting shades of our names for them.[21]

THE WITNESS OF EXTRAVAGANCE

G. K. Chesterton once commented on the strange style of the speech of Jesus. He said, "The diction used about Christ has been, and perhaps wisely, sweet and submissive. But the diction used by Christ is quite curiously gigantesque; it is full of camels leaping through needles and mountains hurled into the sea."[22] Chesterton didn't single out the parables in this connection, but he could have. They are the central specimens of the shocking size of Jesus' speech.

We have already discussed the factor of surprise in most para-bles, how the ordinary keeps bursting into the extraordinary. Now it is time to notice that most of these surprises occur by means of action or event that is extreme. Paul Ricoeur called this phenome-non "the extravagance of the parables," referring to their frequent hyperbole and "outlandishness."[23]

Extravagance takes various forms in the parables. We see it in the recurrent images of growth—seeds yielding great crops in spite of failed plantings (Mark 4:3-8), enemies (Matt 13:24-30), and oddly passive, clueless farmers (Mark 4:26-29). We see it as well in the total divestment of assets for the claiming of a prize—a hidden treasure (Matt 13:44) or a priceless pearl (Matt 13:45). We see it most of all in the central figures of many parables: a father, a Samaritan, a shepherd, certain women, various farmers, landown-ers, masters, and kings. These figures take action of enormous and surreal proportion—the huge gesture, the lavish invitation, the withering or dazzling response. Though in many guises, roles, and moods, all these figures are possessed of a roaring flamboyance. Consistently, they rise to the shocking. At times it's a shocking severity, at times a shocking risk; but most often by something lavish, exuberant, and impossibly grand, these figures astound and strangely expand, their faces filling the sky.

In part, these extremes may serve to arrest our attention, to seize us and shake us from our sleepy, dull assumptions. Flannery O'Connor, with a keen-eyed Catholic faith, filled her short stories and novels with grotesque, bizarre characters and outsized events. She accounted for her strategy this way:

> When you can assume that your audience holds the same beliefs you do, you can relax a little and use more normal ways of talking to it; when you have to assume that it does not, then you have to make your vision apparent by shock—to the hard of hearing you shout, and for the almost-blind you draw large and startling figures.[24]

Jesus drew "large and startling figures," in part, perhaps, because of our near blindness. For our hardness of hearing, the extravagances of the parables are a shout.

More essentially, they bear witness to the size of the mystery that Jesus proclaimed, and to the shocking size of his God. Perhaps this lies at the root of why he told stories less to explain than to perplex, less like illustrations and more like a blow. God is beyond illustration. Jesus' parables did paint pictures, and God was in them; but pictures of God must always be painted too large for a frame, too "other" to be comprehended at a glance. Beyond instructing us or helping us, the stories Jesus told are for reducing us to something like laughter, wonder, fear, and awe.

Perhaps we are invited to one thing more. As we witness these constant crazy moves from the common to the extravagant, from the small to the outrageous, the risky, the beautifully grand, in time it dawns on us that this insistently repeating shift is more than a pattern in parables; it is a way that human lives might come to be lived. Kafka said, "If you only followed the parables you yourselves might become parables."[25] God's best parable was Jesus himself, who told the largest tales and lived the largest life, and kept saying over his shoulder, "Follow me." In those with ears to hear, this Christ isn't finished turning the common and the small into the stunning surprise of parable. Toward these ends, we read, ponder, preach, and follow the parables—and the Parable—of Jesus.

14

THE METHOD OF THIS BOOK

This introductory chapter has sketched in a preliminary way what the parables are, what they seem to intend, and how they do their work. The next eight chapters offer detailed explorations of eight parables. Our study of them will include an ongoing conversation about implications for preaching. My goal is larger than an exegetical/homiletical discussion of eight parables. These parables provide examples of certain features and patterns occurring in many parables. In other words, I have tried to design these chapters as an inductive study of how all the parables might be read and preached. The final chapter, focused on preaching, draws these observations together and offers a summary of principles and strategies.

No texts are richer than these. No preaching is more daunting or more demanding or, in the end, more fulfilling than the preaching of the parables. Not least among the rewards is that the parables themselves have much to teach about how to preach. Closely attending to them can grow us into better preachers of all kinds of texts, and of the gospel itself.

CHAPTER TWO

Someone Scatters Seed

The kingdom of God is as if someone would scatter seed on the ground, and would sleep and rise night and day, and the seed would sprout and grow, he does not know how. The earth produces of itself, first the stalk, then the head, then the full grain in the head. But when the grain is ripe, at once he goes in with his sickle, because the harvest has come. (Mark 4:26-29)

This is hardly the most popular of the parables. Even Matthew and Luke felt free to ignore it. Mark has only a handful of parables, each of them picked up and retold by the other two synoptic evangelists, with the singular exception of this one. Why do they leave it alone? Some modern studies of the parables follow suit, giving it scant notice. The lectionary doesn't even give it a solo position, but pairs it with the parable of the mustard seed. In an oddly appropriate way, this parable seems a bit like the seed of which it tells—small, buried, left alone, unfolding a mystery in secret.

There are serious disagreements about what this parable might mean. Some say it is a parable of patience; others call it a parable of action.[1] Some say the point concerns the farmer, who might stand for God, or for Jesus, or for disciples.[2] Some find the center of meaning in the seed, while others find it in the harvest.[3] The interpretive options are dizzying. So maybe this parable is a good place to begin in asking how we decide what a parable may be trying to say or do.

Preliminary Observations

Consider the context. Our text is one in a cluster of three parables, the first three reported by Mark (4:4-8, 26-29, 30-32). Though these parables have substantial differences in theme and plot, each of them features someone planting seed and an account of what happens to the seed, including some description of growth. The chapter also includes an extended allegorical explanation of the fate of the seeds in the first parable. In thirty verses, Mark plants and grows a lot of seed.

And he speaks of things that are secret. After the first parable, Jesus confides to his disciples: "To you has been given the secret of the kingdom of God." But he speaks in parables to the crowd, he says, "in order that they may indeed look, but not perceive, and may indeed listen, but not understand; so that they may not turn again and be forgiven" (v. 12; cf. Isa 6:9-11). So in Mark's view, these parables carry something concealed from those who do not have "ears to hear" (vv. 9, 23). Is it coincidence that the parables tell of seeds, whose work is done in hiddenness?

Our parable is the first in Mark that refers explicitly to "the kingdom of God." In terms of general makeup, it is rather simple. It has only one character, contains no dialogue or monologue, and spans only four verses. What, then, shall we attend to as we read?

We have already made a fair beginning. We have noticed something about the context in which the parable appears. Jesus' parables need not always be preached with explicit reference to their Gospel contexts. But as we shall see with this parable, the surrounding material in Mark provides useful comparisons, contrasts, and viable clues to meaning.[4]

We have also noticed the field of images presented to us here: seed, earth, planting, growing, harvest. We are in a world of certain smells: the turned earth, the sweet plants. There are colors too: the dark of the soil, the green of young plants, the gold of ripened grain. There is, as well, an arc of time stretching across the sky of this story: a long passage from planting time through meantime to harvesttime. Exegesis of a parable is premature until we have entered its imaginative world.

ATTENDING TO STRUCTURE

A parable's form is in direct relationship with its content. The structure has its way of bearing the message.[5] The structure of this parable is clearly threefold. First, we are shown someone scattering seed. Then, we are shown a passage of time, during which the farmer and the seed do different things. Finally, we are shown the act of harvest.

To consider structure is to notice proportion. Having found three parts in the story, we observe how long the story lingers in each part. In this case, there is a clear disproportion. A word count of the Greek text reveals that the first scene (after "the kingdom of God is as if") takes only seven words, and the third scene uses thirteen; but the middle section uses all of thirty-one. The parable has three parts, but nearly two-thirds of its content occurs in the middle. This corresponds, of course, to the nature of things. Planting and harvest are brief; the growing is long. But the story didn't have to be told in this proportion, and we must assume a deliberate significance in the choice to do so. Rule of thumb: *when any biblical narrative slows its pace, it signals intensified significance.*

Are there other structural clues to meaning? There is some parallel vocabulary. The words *seed* and *earth* occur in sections 1 and 2, and in the same order. In the second section we notice a parallel structure of verbs, the farmer and seed getting two verbs apiece, as if a comparison were being made. Finally, we observe the structure of the verb tenses. The planting in section 1 is in the aorist (past) tense, but all verbs in section 2 are in the present tense. Section 3 returns to an aorist for the ripening, present tense for putting in the sickle, and perfect tense for the harvest having come.

ATTENDING TO LANGUAGE

The language of Jesus is lean. He does not waste words. As Justin said of him, "Brief and concise utterances fell from Him, for He was no sophist, but His Word was the power of God."[6] Obviously, we do not have his exact words. What he spoke in Aramaic passed, for decades, through various filters of the preaching, teaching, and circumstances of early churches, with a radical transposition into the Greek language. But we may assume a certain fidelity on the part of the early church to the patterns of his speech. In fact, this fidelity seems quite evident in the Synoptic Gospels and notably in the parables. The economy of language in them is striking; all seems deliberate. We are left with the impression that each word and each silence may bear significance.[7]

The parable begins, "The kingdom of God is as if someone [*anthrōpos*, human being] would scatter [*balē*, throw] seed on the ground." This vocabulary is quite general and nonspecific to farming. Contrast Mark's first parable, which uses very different vocabulary for the same action. There "a sower [*speirōn*] went out to sow [*speirai*]" (4:3). By designation, he *is* a planter of seed, and he goes out planting seeds. Our parable, on the other hand, features, vaguely, someone throwing seeds. This character is introduced with a shrug.

And then he goes to sleep. "And would sleep and rise night and day," says the text. This is odd. Many scholars explain that we are told first of his sleeping because the Jewish day begins at sundown, so the first business of the day is to sleep. While this may be fact, it does not account for the language here or for its startling effect. The words collide. God's reign is as if someone would throw seed and sleep.

The full clause, of course, is meant to indicate the farmer's continuing life while the seed grows. But notice the silences. No mention is made of any work on the crop. What farmer does nothing to assist his planted field? Even more strange, there is no mention of his doing anything else either. Why not say something like "and he went about his business day and night"? Not this fellow; he just goes to bed and gets up again, for months. The story's refusal to give him better verbs makes him comic. As David Buttrick says, "Most of the farmers Jesus describes are truly dumb."[8]

In contrast to the farmer's odd passiveness, the seeds are jumping. While he "sleeps and rises," they "sprout and grow." With that, the narrative suddenly stops, and we are given a peek inside this farmer's head. We are told, "He does not know how." Well, of course, he doesn't. No one comprehends the marvel of a seed erupting into root and sprout, pushing out of itself. We are in the presence of a mystery. It seems appropriate that the Greek word for the farmer's not knowing is *oiden*, which has the sense of seeing. He does not see how. The mystery is hidden from his seeing/knowing. The parable has paused to underline his ignorance, and ours.

What follows is a declaration of the mystery: "The earth produces of itself." The word for "of itself" is *automatē*, from which English derives *automatic*. It is the first word of the sentence in the Greek text, giving it an emphatic position. The word has several uses in the Septuagint, including references to volunteer plants. In Leviticus 25 it occurs twice, referring both times to grain growing in a field that is not planted, first in the sabbatical year, then in the jubilee year (vv. 5, 11). In both cases, the grain is not to be harvested. Some scholars find in the use of this word a hint of sabbatical or jubilee themes, but this could be only in an obliquely metaphorical sense,[9] as the seed in the parable is planted and its produce harvested.

Notice a fascinating connection to the earlier parable in which the sowing of seeds gets four different results (4:3-8). Three failures are reported there, and each one is clearly explained. Some seed fell on the path and went to the birds; some fell on rock and withered; some fell among thorns and were choked. Commenting on that parable, Crossan observes, "While the precise methods and reasons of failure are clearly spelled out, the precise modes of success are not detailed in any way. We know what makes bad soil bad (path, rocks, thorns) but what makes good soil good?"[10] The automatic earth is a mystery.

And see what it makes of the seed: "first the stalk, then the head, then the full grain in the head." Nineteenth-century scholars loved this. Under the sway of a cheerful evolutionary optimism, they waved this text like a banner for the marching "progress" of the kingdom of God. What we surely have here instead is a further invitation to consider the mystery. Up until now, the parable has offered certain declarations about the mystery: while a farmer does nothing, seeds sprout and grow; he can't see how; the earth just does it. Now the parable pauses in a new way to say, *See* this! This brief, vivid scene functions like one of those time-lapse nature films of a growing plant. In seconds we are shown all the changes; the effect is dramatic.

The description is not necessary to the parable's plot, so why is it here? It adds the delight of vividness, brightening the wonder reported in the tale. (The RSV works better on this count than the

NRSV. In "first the blade, then the ear, then the full grain in the ear," we see moist greens and golds; "stalks" and "heads" seem dry brown.) These words also give a linguistic sense of growth. Much as in the earlier double-triad in 4:8, "growing up and increasing and yielding thirty and sixty and a hundredfold," the language itself is performing the growth it describes. This is good story-telling.

The last verse comprises the final scene. Harvest is a natural con-clusion to the story, but certainty about the tone and weight of the scene is difficult. The words "he goes in with his sickle, because the harvest has come" are reminiscent of Joel 3:13, part of a fierce ora-cle about God's apocalyptic war on the nations. The same language appears in Revelation 14:15, 18. For some interpreters the violence of these apocalyptic texts carries weight in the parable. In Scott's view, a deliberate tension has been introduced to force reflection on whether the kingdom of God is gracious like the parable's overall tone, or violent as in Joel's vision.[11] This dynamic may be in play, but it seems too subtle to be at the center of what the parable is doing.

Other scholars focus on the final scene by claiming that the para-ble is all about the contrast between the farmer's decisive (eschato-logical) action and his earlier inactivity.[12] Certainly, the "harvest" was a metaphor in Israel for the last days, and the parable surely presents a contrast between the farmer's long idleness and his sud-den action. But, again, is this a real point of emphasis? Linguistic markers for this contrast are not strong. Though English transla-tions begin verse 29 with "but," the Greek word is not the strongly contrastive *alla* but the weaker *de*, which can even mean "and." "Suddenly" *(euthus)* sounds like a contrast, but Mark is so fond of that word (this is its nineteenth use), it seems to be a stylistic quirk.

The final verse has three clauses, but only the first and the last have nouns. The first noun is *karpos* (fruit), and echoes the earlier line, "the earth produces [*karpophorei*, bears fruit] of itself." The noun in the second clause, "harvest," appears fittingly and dra-matically as the final word of the parable. Syntactically, the action of the man lies in between. There may even be an implied subordi-nation of his role to that of the fruit. Though the NRSV says, "When the grain is ripe," the verb is *paradoi* (gives over) and is in subjunc-tive, not passive, mode. The sense of the expression is "when the fruit allows." So even as the farmer goes into action at last, it is the mystery that allows him.

FREEDOM, ONCE MORE

Before considering how to preach this text, we should observe two features in it that are typical of Jesus' parables. Both features pertain to something slippery, which we have earlier called the parables' freedom.

First, notice the parable's resistance to allegory. We naturally want to equate the seed-thrower with God or Jesus or even the church, but when we seize on any one of these choices, the parable squirms out of our grasp. Does any of these three "fit" a figure who plants, does nothing else, does not know how, then puts in the (eschatological) sickle? No. Trying to draw neat equations from a parable can be maddening. This one requires us to give it up.

And notice the parable's resistance to any single meaning. Interpreters often advocate a single meaning, but any one choice seems too small here. Is Jesus declaring that the reign of God is presently hidden but will one day be manifest, or that it used to be hidden and is now a visible harvest? Is he giving comfort to those who see no signs, or is he warning those who think their efforts can bring in the kingdom? Is he urging us to be patient or to be prepared or simply to celebrate the great mystery? Candor requires us to shake our heads and to sigh, if not to laugh. Who can say what it means?[13]

In a way, it's like a joke. A joke doesn't have a meaning; it has an impact. Dissect it and it dies on the table. Frederick Buechner has said:

> Though we have approached these parables reverently all these many years and have heard them expounded as grave and reverent vehicles of truth, I suspect that many if not all of them were originally not grave at all but were antic, comic.... I suspect that Jesus spoke many of his parables as a kind of sad and holy joke and that that may be part of why he seemed reluctant to explain them because if you have to explain a joke, you might as well save your breath.[14]

The parable before us is surely something like a joke. It's not hard to read it as one: "God's reign is like this guy who throws seed on the ground and goes to sleep and gets up, night and day. The seed sprouts and grows—the guy doesn't have a clue. The dirt just produces—blade, ear, grain. When the fruit allows, the guy goes to work; it's a harvest."

The question is, how do you preach a joke?

HOMILETICAL REFLECTIONS

If you are a lectionary preacher, you should make a choice between this parable and the one about the mustard seed with which it is paired. There are some parallels between them, but they are doing quite different things. What's more, the mustard parable shows up again in Year A, which should give our parable the edge for Year B. Preach it by itself.

Since the parable doesn't make a single point but functions through a sequence of developments and surprises to make a certain impact and suggest a range of implications, the sermon should seek to do the same. This will be true of preaching any parable. The story should be walked through. Instead of telling it first, then leaving it to expound on various "points," consider unfolding the whole sermon along the sequence of the story, pausing here and there to reflect and respond.

Still, the sermon must have focus. For all the levels of meaning that may be present in the parable, the preacher must decide where the greater weight of it seems to lie, or the sermon becomes a ramble. The choice emerges from the kind of careful study we have done, and will give rise to the sermon's priorities, order, and tone.

My reading of the parable shows repeated indicators that significant weight is placed on an altogether potent and hilarious mystery. The midsection of the story, showing the activity of the seed/earth/plants and the idleness of the farmer, is by far the largest. Two breaks from the narrative—"he does not know how" and "the earth produces of itself"—seem to underline the mystery. So does the tone, which at one point offers mirth (he throws seed and sleeps and nothing else?), and elsewhere offers visual, rhythmic delight (first the blade, then the ear, then the full grain in the ear). As we have seen, there are also elements in the first and last scenes that seem to underplay the farmer's role. We also have in the larger context a theme of hiddenness, and these words to the disciples: "To you has been given the *musterion*" (secret or mystery).

These indicators are certainly not to be lined up and explicated in the sermon. We won't be trying to build a case! But they have yielded what seems to be a center of gravity[15] and a primary tone of the parable and of our sermon.

The sermon can follow the parable in how it plays. As the story is playful with the farmer, so are we. As it delights in watching the plants grow, so may we. Why not show the sprouts pushing out of the dirt like little green fists, the farmer looking out the window from his bed, yawning, scratching, speaking in monotone to the wife, "Corn's up." Or we can imagine a different kind of farmer, dumber than this one, trying to take charge of the mystery, pacing up and down the field with a megaphone chanting, "Grow! Grow! Grow!" or kneeling over the sprouts to pull their little leaves higher. Follow the parable's play.

The tone and delivery of this sermon should be, like the parable, nonanxious. If the preacher is tense or grave or shouting or show-ing signs of literary overachievement, the story of a relaxed farmer and the spontaneous earth, even if told, will never arrive in the room. The teller can drown out the tale. A preacher is wise to ask: How may I embody the parable?

Which leads to the necessary prior question of where the parable connects with the preacher's life. This one could connect at several points. Despairing over slow or nonexistent progress in "the work"?—Take heart, God's reign is like buried seed. Getting a bit complacent?—Watch out, the future comes like a sudden harvest. But perhaps the parable's fullest connection for preachers will be precisely at the point we have identified as central in the story, the mystery beyond our management.

We may think of ourselves as religious professionals, but we're just people throwing seed. We may think of preaching as a science or an art, but for all our most savvy efforts, we're up there moving our mouths about matters we can't comprehend. We train our-selves in "church management," but the power of God will do what it will, and is quite pleased to do so without us. To know this is to come closer to redemption. Andrew Harvey said, "We are saved in the end by the things that ignore us."[16] I can think of no tribe in greater need of that word than those of us who preach the gospel. To know such a word would send us into the pulpit freer, less anxious about ourselves, less inclined to take constant measurements, less needy of affirmation, more at ease in the potent and finally hilarious mystery of God. That is not only how to preach this parable; it is how this parable teaches us to preach.

CHAPTER THREE

Two Men Went Up to the Temple

Two men went up to the temple to pray, one a Pharisee and the other a tax collector. The Pharisee, standing by himself, was praying thus, "God, I thank you that I am not like other people: thieves, rogues, adulterers, or even like this tax collector. I fast twice a week; I give a tenth of all my income." But the tax collector, standing far off, would not even look up to heaven, but was beating his breast and saying, "God, be merciful to me, a sinner!" I tell you, this man went down to his home justified rather than the other. (Luke 18:10-14a)

In the previous chapter we explored a parable that nicely posed some introductory questions about how to read and preach a parable. The parable before us now raises a more specific and treacherous problem. We may call it the problem of identification, which might be recognized as follows:

Suppose that on a given Sunday you are a visitor in a church. The Gospel reading turns out to be the parable of the Pharisee and the tax collector. Consulting the worship bulletin, you see a sermon title that leaves no doubt—you are about to hear a sermon on this parable. Now ask yourself: *Am I stirred with a sense of curiosity, anticipation, eagerness? Do I lean forward for this one?* Or are you perhaps thinking, *Here we go again?* Don't you know exactly what the sermon will say? And isn't it because this parable is so clear-cut and obvious, with a moral that no one can miss?

It's as if the parable of the Pharisee and the tax collector were somehow like Aesop's fable "The Tortoise and the Hare." Now

27

how would you preach that? Describe the braggart rabbit flaunting his speed against the poor, lowly turtle. Tell how the rabbit rested on his laurels while the turtle plodded on. Then give the moral: "Slow and steady wins the race," and come up with three ways this is true. Pontificate, stir, and serve.

Actually, the fable provides a perfect contrast to the way our parable works. The fable works by means of two kinds of *distance* from the hearer. There is first the distance of characters that are not like us—in this case animals with one-dimensional attributes. There is also a distance in the plot, an unrealistic and unambiguous conflict, in no way complex or confusing, as real conflicts usually are. From this distance created by artificial characters and plot, a simple didactic lesson appears—in short, a moral.

We find an obvious moral in our parable only because we view it in the same way as the fable. We see the two characters as one-dimensional, not like us; and we see the plot as cut-and-dried. These distancing assumptions distort the story from parable to fable. The key to experiencing this parable, and to preaching it, is identification. We will need to identify with the characters as three-dimensional figures like ourselves, and therefore to identify with the plot as disturbing.

CONTEXT

Jesus is on his way to Jerusalem, where the parable itself is set. We are near the end of Luke's long travel narrative (9:51–19:27), during which he has departed from Mark's outline and drawn from a sayings source (Q) and from his own materials (L). Our parable is the last material from Luke's own source before he returns to Mark's outline. Perhaps the culminating position gives it special weight.[1]

Or perhaps we should say that the *two* parables concluding Luke's own material in the travel narrative carry special weight. Just preceding our text is the parable of a widow pestering an unjust judge for justice (18:2-5). Luke often places complementary stories side by side with male figures in one and female figures in the other (cf. 1:8-23/26-38; 1:46-55/67-79; 7:1-10/11-17; 10:25-37/38-42; 13:18-19/20-21; 15:3-7/8-10). Both parables here present two urban characters set against each other. Luke says the first is *about* prayer, while the second shows two people *at* prayer. The widow becomes a model of feisty prayer and the tax collector a model of lowly prayer, a nice balance in itself. John Donahue puts both parables under the rubric "Trial by Prayer."[2]

But the more profound link between the two parables is the theme of *vindication*.[3] In the first, what the widow demands (v. 3), what the judge finally grants (v. 5), and what Jesus twice says God will do for the elect (vv. 7-8) is to "vindicate" *(ekdikeō)*. In addition to a fourfold use of this verb, the judge is described with the same Greek root, *adikias*, "unjust" (v. 6). The same language appears in our parable: it is told to "some who trusted in themselves that they were *dikaioi*" (v. 9, NRSV: "righteous"); the Pharisee refers to *adikoi* (v. 11, NRSV: "rogues"); the tax collector goes home *dedikaiomenos* (v. 14, NRSV: "justified"). English resorts to an assortment of semantically unrelated words to render these variations of a single Greek root, but clearly, the widow and the tax collector are granted the same thing. Fred Craddock suggests that the two parables present a certain balance in this regard. The first becomes an assurance to the "elect" who cry to God for justice—"Yes, God will accomplish the great reversal." The second becomes a warning—"Be careful lest you yourselves become victims of that reversal."[4]

STRUCTURE

On either side of the parable, Luke sets an interpretive frame. He reports that it was spoken "to some who trusted in themselves that they were righteous and regarded others with contempt" (v. 9). These words are a mixed blessing. They predispose us against the Pharisee and thereby remove us from Jesus' listeners, who got to puzzle through the parable for themselves. On the other hand, "to some who" might well include people other than Pharisees. Immediately after the parable, the disciples turn children away from Jesus, proving that they are among those who "regarded others with contempt."[5] At the end of the parable Luke adds an interpretive conclusion, again in general terms: "for all who exalt themselves will be humbled, but all who humble themselves will be exalted" (v. 14*b*).[6]

The structure of the parable itself is simple. It begins with two men going up to the temple and ends with them going back down.

The order in which they are mentioned, however, becomes reversed. In the going up, the Pharisee is first; in the going down, the tax collector is first. Within this frame lies the central section of the parable, in which each man in turn is observed in a parallel structure: first a description of the man, then his prayer, beginning with the word *God*. In each case we see the man before hearing him.

Though the structure is parallel, the proportions are uneven. The prayer of the Pharisee is longer than that of the tax collector (twenty-nine words to six in the Greek text); but the description of the tax collector is longer than that of the Pharisee (twenty words to seven). Inside the temple, the Pharisee gets a total of eight more words than the tax collector; but in their departure, the tax collector gets nine words and the Pharisee only two. Even the proportions of language embody the great reversal.

God gets no words, but is a presence nonetheless, the veiled but central figure. The two framing scenes of the parable bear indirect reference to God, in scene 1 by means of the temple and prayer, in scene 3 by the verb "having been justified," behind which God is the unnamed agent. In the central scene, God is named twice, once on the lips of each man. In a story with two characters in the same place at the same time, both of whom speak, it is striking that neither speaks to the other. All speech is addressed to God, who, though silent and hidden in the narrative, decides all outcomes.

HEARING THE PARABLE

In Greek the parable's first word is *anthrōpoi*—"persons." Two persons go up to the temple to pray. Soon we will see many differences between them, but at first mention they are equally persons.[7] Though the text indicates nothing concerning the time of their arrival, Jesus' hearers may well have assumed that the occasion was one of the two daily services, at 9:00 and at 3:00.

The biases we hold against Pharisees were not shared by Jesus' hearers. Pharisees were lay leaders with exceptional commitments. In an era of imperial oppression and encroaching pluralism, their exemplary lives held the vital faith of Israel together and continued to do so after the nation was destroyed. Their sacrifices were considerable. Their reasons for opposing the radical claims of Jesus are understandable, yet not all of them opposed him. Luke tells of three Pharisees who opened their homes to him (7:36; 11:37; 14:1) and of some who tried to save him from Herod (13:31). Saul of Tarsus was not the only Pharisee to join the Jesus movement (Acts 15:5). We do best to join with Jesus' hearers and see the Pharisees through appreciative eyes.

The tax collector is another matter. As Gerhard Ebeling said, "The New Testament tax collector has been for us covered with a religious patina almost surrounded by a halo."[8] Familiar with all the happy notices about Jesus and tax collectors, we already like this man. But consider the truth about him. He has struck a deal with the empire. His title is *toll* collector.[9] On top of the heavy poll taxes and land taxes Rome already levied, it claimed "indirect" taxes—customs, duties, tariffs, tolls—and he has volunteered for the job. He sits in a booth, takes money from his own oppressed people to give to the empire, and takes extra to line his pockets. He is both traitor and extortionist, a certified leech. A man who made such arrangements with Gentiles might easily have other doubtful involvements, as suggested by the Gospels' regular linking of tax collectors, prostitutes, and sinners (Mark 2:15-16, par.; Matt 11:19, par., 21:31-32).

Jesus' listeners would have found the opening line of the parable jarring. Crossan gives a nice equivalent: "A Pope and a pimp went into St. Peter's to pray." He goes on to say, "No matter where the story goes after such an opening, the narrator has placed himself in jeopardy by the initial juxtaposition."[10]

Having been told first of the Pharisee, we now observe him. There is textual and exegetical disagreement about whether he is standing "by himself" or praying "to" or "about himself." Reading that he stands by himself provides a parallel with verse 13, which tells where the tax collector stood.[11]

His prayer is a thanksgiving. We may judge the Pharisee as trusting in himself (v. 9), but Jesus shows him "in the very act of giving God the glory."[12] As every commentary on the parables observes, it reflects a form of prayer that was neither uncommon nor reprehensible.[13] What is wrong with thanking God for having been spared an ungodly life and for the privilege of living in obedience to divine command?

In fact, he exceeds divine command. The Torah prescribes one fast per year, on the Day of Atonement; but he deprives himself of food and water from sunrise to sunset every Monday and Thursday, a penitential act in behalf of the nation. Tithing all his income also goes beyond Torah's command. Not only were certain kinds of produce exempt, but any purchased produce need not be tithed, since it was already to be tithed by the producer. But this man leaves nothing to chance, nothing unblessed by the sacrament of giving to God. The prayer need not be deemed self-righteous. He is thanking *God* for the life he is able to lead.

Still, there is, at its very center, a discordant note. Having thanked God that he is not like people who are thieves, rogues, and adulterers, he sharpens his focus to a specific man: "or even like this tax collector." Perhaps the telling word is *this (houtos)*. It is a distancing, isolating word. The earlier notice that he stood "by himself" acquires new significance. More, his mention of a fellow worshiper gives the suggestion of a sidelong glance. It's as if he has stopped praying and gone to peeking.

The toll collector, by contrast, looks downward. Abandoning the common posture of prayer (face and hands lifted), he "would not even look up to heaven, but was beating his breast." Add to this that he was "standing far off," and we see a kind of triple shrinking in this man: head down, arms in, physical distance from the altar. Especially notable is the beating of the breast, an act of extreme agitation and grief. It was most commonly done by women.[14] Notice, too, that whereas the Pharisee is "praying," the tax collector is "saying." All things religious seem lost to him.

His prayer begins exactly like the Pharisee's, *ho theos*, but bears no other resemblance. Only four words follow—a choked petition. *Hilastheti* (be merciful) is a rare verb with connections to atonement (cf. Heb 2:17). Its significance may be heightened here if the occasion is one of the two daily services of atonement sacrifice. In Kenneth Bailey's words, the toll collector's cry might mean something like, "Let it be for me! Make an atonement for me, a sinner!"[15] Though the Pharisee's prayer is often called self-centered, it is more the toll collector whose prayer concerns himself. The Pharisee refers to those he is not like and to what he does. The toll collector's self-reference is to who he *is*, "the sinner."

How we are to feel about this prayer isn't entirely clear, but quite possibly we are to hear it as pathetic. It carries not a word of concrete repentance, no indication of intended change. Zacchaeus is a proper model of repentance, committing himself to reparations (Luke 19:8). Imagine him at the foot of the sycamore beating his chest, mumbling, "Have mercy!"—and saying nothing more. But the toll collector's prayer offers nothing by way of restoring ill-gotten gain or otherwise amending his life.

So it is all the more stunning when Jesus declares, "I tell you, this man went down to his home justified rather than the other."[16] Several points are worth making about this language. First, there is an ironic repetition of a word used earlier by the Pharisee. "This [*houtos*] tax collector," he had said. Yes, says Jesus, "this [*houtos*] went to his home justified." (English adds "man," which does not appear in the Greek.) Second, it might have been said that he went home "forgiven," but the word *justified* (made righteous) is used in a deliberate reversal of the righteousness mentioned in verse 9.[17] Finally, while we are told that "this one went to his home," there is no mention of where the Pharisee went, as if he has no place to go that matters.

HOMILETICAL REFLECTIONS

David Buttrick is correct in saying that this parable is as hard to preach as any.[18] We want to make it neater than it is. We might wish, for example, to say that it means God rejects the proud and justifies the penitent. Luke's framing of the story (vv. 9, 14*b*) invites this conclusion. But both men are ambiguous; there is good in the Pharisee, and the toll collector's penitence is incomplete. Should we really say that God justifies people or not depending on what words and feelings they pray? The parable is surely not an invitation to keep ourselves in a never-ending state of breast-beating penitence.[19]

So maybe we wish to say the point is really that God justifies by grace alone, that the temple indicates a center of sacred surprise in which the world's values are turned upside down by One who grandly bestows goodness on the least likely. Well, yes, but this, too, is not enough, for the parable does make a point of the Pharisee's separating himself from the toll collector. Whatever else the parable suggests, passing judgment on others is one of its concerns. So is the value of seeking repentance.

It seems to me wise to recall that the parable's center is God. God is the One who acts to justify this badly flawed person and not that one. The parable refuses to tell us why, leaves us wondering at the mystery of God's implausible choices. This, I think, should be the central impact of a sermon on this text.

But the whole untidy tale must be told, in which a good man disparages a bad man and a bad man makes poor penance. The story invites us to see ourselves in both. It invites us to our own imperfect seeking to be made right and, as we do, to stop separating ourselves from others. In it all, we are to trust God's freedom to justify the worst folks—suspecting that this means us, and willing to bet that the surest way to lose the great surprise is to withhold it from anyone else.

Strategically, the most important task of a sermon on this parable is identification. Our problem is distance. At the usual distance from this parable, the Pharisee and the toll collector appear as flat as two cartoon characters on a screen. One is a poor bum down on his luck; the other is a sanctimonious creep. From our seats we can all sit back and enjoy the cartoon, and when it's over sing a chorus of "God, we thank you we're not like this Pharisee!" For the parable to have any chance with us, we must make the imaginative and candid choice to come forward, to step behind the cartoon curtain and into the story. Jesus told the parable to people who knew Pharisees and toll collectors as rounded, real people. So we stand as close as we can to these rounded men and search their eyes for reflections of our faces.

How do we achieve such identification in the sermon? One way, of course, is to relate some facts, as we have done in this chapter. Given especially the insidious view of Pharisees (and by extension Judaism) that has been propagated by Christians, there is really no way around this. Some of the essential knowledge held by the first hearers of the parable must be reclaimed for the hearers of the sermon. Tell the historical truth.

But this won't be enough. Using historical data in a sermon to "explain" a text has two limitations. First, too much of it will simply bog down a sermon. We begin to sound like a documentary. Scintillating as our research may be to us, the congregation hasn't shown up in hopes of becoming better Near Eastern historians. Second, such explanations easily keep the parable in the past, which is another way of keeping ourselves at a comfortable distance.

For these reasons, our necessary comments on Pharisees and toll collectors are offered briefly. And instead of starting the sermon in the present day, then whisking us off to first-century Palestine, then hauling us back again to the present, we keep the parable and the people in the room. Historical references should be brief, and they should be integrated with the present.

One way to do this is by means of deliberate anachronism, playfully mixing the practices of past and present. We might say of the Pharisee, for instance, "Twice a week this man goes without food. He tithes on everything and is glad that he can. He teaches Sunday school, visits the hospitals, helps feed the hungry." In these lines, we have consciously overlaid past and present to keep the dynamic of the parable at work. Notice not only the use of anachronism (Sunday school, hospital visits) but also a preference for simple, contemporary speech and the use of the present tense.

We might even go farther by imagining certain additional details of the story. Something like this, for example:

> What the parable neglects to mention is that the Pharisee on the way to church that day was singing, "Amazing grace, how sweet the sound." And that while he is praying, there are tears in his eyes—he *feels* his thanks. And if we ask him on his way out what he thinks of the tax collector, he will say, "There but for the grace of God go I"— and he will mean it.
>
> What the parable also neglects to point out is that the tax collector, when he has wiped his eyes and blown his nose and gone home, will not be quitting his shady job. He can't see any options. It's a nasty business, but he's stuck in it. Tomorrow he'll take the money again from his neighbors, hand it over to the empire, and put some aside for himself.

Passages like these can introduce the kind of tensions apparently intended by the parable, and they do so by staying in narrative mode, not resorting to explanatory discourse.

Jürgen Moltmann uses a more straightforward device in a sermon. After the introduction, which is a balance between well-expressed historical description and an insistence that the parable is about us, Moltmann goes on to say that he will no longer use the words *Pharisee* and *tax collector*, but will speak simply of "the good man" and "the bad man."[20] This is yet another way to translate foreign figures and distant terms into the pressingly relevant drama that the parable is.

Not least of the possibilities for preaching this parable is that its setting, uniquely, is the same as the setting for the sermon itself. All who hear (or preach) the sermon have come up to the temple to pray. In the course of the liturgy, all will express thanks like the Pharisee and confession like the tax collector. As in the parable, these will be offered by flawed people in flawed ways. And as in the parable, the central figure of the hour, silent as light, will judge and bless, cleansing the temple once more.[21] God's verdicts aren't spoken here, but they are on us as we leave, and in all cases have the power to lead us home, made right.

CHAPTER FOUR

From Jerusalem to Jericho

A man was going down from Jerusalem to Jericho, and fell into the hands of robbers, who stripped him, beat him, and went away, leaving him half dead. Now by chance a priest was going down that road; and when he saw him, he passed by on the other side. So likewise a Levite, when he came to the place and saw him, passed by on the other side. But a Samaritan while traveling came near him; and when he saw him, he was moved with pity. He went to him and bandaged his wounds, having poured oil and wine on them. Then he put him on his own animal, brought him to an inn, and took care of him. The next day he took out two denarii, gave them to the innkeeper, and said, "Take care of him; and when I come back, I will repay you whatever more you spend." (Luke 10:30-35)

This much-loved parable is by no means simple. It requires five characters plus a gang of bandits and a beast. Its plot includes five scenes and the promise of a sixth. And as given by Luke, the parable itself is a scene within another narrative plot, a story within the story of Jesus and a certain lawyer. Inside that larger story, the parable works like a buried explosive—the stunning narrative surprise shakes and shifts the ground of the lawyer's perspective, and our own. Robert Funk may well be correct when he writes, "There is no other parable in the Jesus tradition that carries a comparable punch."[1]

THE FRAME STORY BEGUN (vv. 25-29)

The parable is set within a frame that adds its own dynamic to the tale. It is difficult to imagine preaching the parable apart from the story that frames it. The two stories are set in tight counterpoint.[2] The parable erupts from its context like a springing leopard.

Just prior to the lawyer's appearance, Jesus has spoken of the great reversal—outsiders turned to insiders and vice versa. Hearing the exuberant report of the seventy, just returned from their mission, he thanks God: "because you have hidden these things from the wise and the intelligent and have revealed them to infants" (10:21).

"And look *[kai idou]*," says Luke, "a lawyer stood up." Clearly, he is one of "the wise and the intelligent," a professional in the application of Torah. Intending to "test" Jesus, he asks, "Teacher, what must I do to inherit eternal life?" (v. 25). The question, apparently, is hollow. Though one might "test" any rabbi's teaching quite sincerely by seeking his answer to a fundamental question, Luke's report that the lawyer's follow-up question was "to justify himself" suggests that he was posing from the start. As in so much religious talk, he isn't asking the ultimate questions; he is fondling them.

The lawyer's question is met with a counterquestion: "What is written in the law? What do you read there?" Jesus has turned it back on him. It is worth pointing out that to such a question as the lawyer's, Jesus would never resort to parable. Both the question and the answer are too basic for indirect discourse. The way to life is clearly set forth in the Torah; the questioner already knows it. One recalls the final speech of Moses to Israel: "Surely, this commandment that I am commanding you today is not too hard for you, nor is it too far away. It is not in heaven.... Neither is it beyond the sea.... No, the word is very near to you; it is in your mouth and in your heart for you to observe" (Deut 30:11-14). Some older lectionaries actually link this text to our parable, though the Revised Common Lectionary does not.

The lawyer complies with the answer to his own question. It is a merging of the Shema's command to love God entirely (Deut 6:5) and the command of the Holiness Code to love one's neighbor as oneself (Lev 19:18). In parallel accounts (Mark 12:28-31; Matt 22:34-40), it is Jesus who joins these two great commands. Luke would have us recall that such insight was already held in Israel.[3] Jesus here does not instruct a student of Torah but confirms him: "You have given the right answer; do this, and you will live." As Luke repeatedly insists, from his first scene of a Torah-keeping priestly couple, Zechariah and Elizabeth (1:5-6), to his last scene of disciples "continually in the temple" (24:53), Jesus and his way are in perfect continuity with Israel's faith.

The dialogue to this point presents the following pattern: the lawyer asks a question; Jesus asks a counterquestion; the lawyer gives an answer; Jesus gives a counteranswer. In what follows, the pattern is repeated. The lawyer asks a question ("And who is my neighbor?"); Jesus asks a counterquestion (the parable + "Which of these three, do you think, was a neighbor . . . ?"); the lawyer gives an answer ("The one who showed him mercy"); Jesus gives a counteranswer ("Go and do likewise").[4] Notice other similarities in the repeated pattern. To both of the lawyer's questions is added an ascription of negative motive. Both of Jesus' counterquestions use pointed second-person verbs ("What do you read there?" "Which do you think?"). Both of Jesus' counteranswers, affirming the lawyer's reply, are imperatives to "do" it ("Do [*poiei*] this and you will live"; "Go and do [*poiei*] likewise").

Though the lawyer's motive is "to justify himself," his question "And who is my neighbor?" has more objective merit than we might think. No one could ask such a question for whom love is a dreamy abstraction. If love is a nice fuzzy feeling, one can easily say, "I just love everybody!" But if love means concrete action, expending actual resources on real people—that is, if love is taken seriously—then one might well ask where the boundaries are. With pressing needs everywhere and limited resources, are we not forced to choose whose needs to serve? So the lawyer's question was, in fact, a debated issue of the day. "Neighbor" in Leviticus 19 refers to one's own people, and yet the same chapter also commands love for "the stranger who sojourns with you" (Lev 19:33-34 RSV). But now, in 30 C.E., Judea is overrun with "strangers," among whom the faithful are under many forms of threat. When your own people are oppressed, the command to love your neighbor as yourself takes on a new pathos; and the question "Who is my neighbor?" is ethically real.

But Jesus seems unimpressed with the question. He counters with a parable that turns it completely on its head.[5] One gets the impression that before he opens his mouth, there is a weighty silence, a sharp gaze, the charged air that precedes lightning.

THE PARABLE

The story has its coordinates on an actual landscape. The road from Jerusalem to Jericho was solidly real to Jesus' hearers. It was a road with a reputation. First-century writers described it as a wild place, with violent men close by.[6] The road was seventeen miles long—a steep climb toward Jerusalem, a steep descent toward Jericho—a sharply turning, desolate, dangerous trek.

Down that curving, rugged road, "a certain person [*anthrōpos tis*]" was descending. All other characters in the parable will be described in terms of their social location, but the traveler is given no descriptors at all (though certainly he is a Jewish male). He could, therefore, be anyone. We may see him as a kind of Everyone—not in the allegorical sense, but in the sense that the narrative's choice to leave him undescribed invites universal identification.

True to the road's reputation, violence erupts upon the traveler. He falls among bandits who abuse him, as described in a fast flurry of four verbs. The text reports their actions in forceful participles: stripping him, striking blows on him, going off, leaving him half dead. The verbs point to their cruelty. Their beating of the man (with clubs, fists, feet?) occurs after they have humiliated him and made him defenseless by stripping him. It is the picture of sense-less, murderous group violence. Knowing the road's reputation, we might have anticipated trouble, but the brutal details sober us. This man, reduced to our common nakedness and on the brink of our common death, is a figure now of the most elemental and raw human need.

Is the story crafted so as to invite our identification with this man? Quite possibly. Robert Funk has championed this position.[7] He argues that the parable's point of view is that of the victim, that its hearers "take up a vantage point in the ditch to await develop-ments."[8] Funk's claim has merit. The traveler is the only character present in every scene of the parable. He is a blank slate, not only undescribed but silent throughout. The vicious details of his assault elicit our sympathy. Like him and with him, we wait to see who will come to help. If our preference is to identify not with him but with his rescuer, the story frustrates us. The rescuer turns out to be someone with whom it is impossible to identify: an enemy. The only character whose position we can finally claim is the one who *needs* a neighbor.

So we take our place by the wounded man to see who will come by. Sure enough, here comes someone, a priest. We are told that his appearance is "by chance" or "by coincidence" *(kata sugkurian)*. The implication of this expression is not clear. It could be a piece of storytelling flare, as in, "Now it just so happened." Hedrick reads it as a secular notice that no benevolent providence is at work for the wounded traveler, that his fate could go either way.[9] Nolland takes it to mean something like "as luck would have it," setting up an expectation that the presence of a priest on the road is good fortune for the victim.[10]

The priest's direction of travel is the same as the victim's had been; he is "going down," headed for Jericho, his back to Jerusalem. Presumably, he has finished a term of service at the temple and is headed home. Jericho was, in fact, the home of many priests. We are told that when he came to the place where the victim lay, "he saw him [and] passed by on the other side." Discussions abound concerning his reasons for giving wide berth to a half-dead man. Assuming that the victim appears to be dead, texts are adduced on the defilement incurred in touching a corpse (Lev 21:1-2, 11).[11] Counterarguments are made from the Talmud, which stipulate that an *abandoned* corpse must be attended to, even by a priest.[12] These discussions of priestly obligation provide interesting background, but their importance for hearing the parable is doubtful. The parable is silent on what laws the priest is keeping or breaking. They are irrelevant.

Down the same path now comes a Levite, a cleric of lesser rank. His response to the victim is described in exact parallel to the response of the priest: he "saw him [and] passed by on the other side."

With this development, something about the shape of the parable becomes clear. Like so many folktales, fairy tales, and jokes, it uses "the rule of three." The pattern is familiar. A situation is repeated three times with three characters. The third provides resolution, and our expectation of the third is set up by the first two. There are clues in the parable that this age-old formula is in play. The parallel language—both men "saw him" and "passed by on the other side"—constitutes such a clue. So does the terseness of each account. The story's quick dispatch of these two seems almost dismissive (as they were dismissive), eager to show us another. We are not surprised. We don't expect the clergy to be of much use, and we don't expect Jesus to feature clergy as heroes. But most of all, *this is a tale*; we know there will be three, that the first two will get it wrong, and the third will get it right.

But notice the trap that has been set. In "the rule of three" the first two characters establish expectation for the third. If the first two figures differ from each other, we expect the third to represent another difference on the same continuum (an Irishman, an Englishman—an American). If the first two are of the same type, we expect the third figure to represent an opposite type (two lazy pigs—an industrious pig). This parable operates in the latter form. In the priest and the Levite, Jesus has dealt us two of a kind. Both are clergy; both are useless. We now lean forward, ready for a third character opposite in type and in response to the victim. We have been set up to expect, in other words, a helpful *layperson*. The opposite of clergy is laity or, in the terminology of first-century Palestine, an "Israelite."[13]

The figure that approaches instead is, incongruously, a Samaritan. His appearance is a riveting shock. The story's categories have been totally altered. The working category till now was religion: priest, Levite—layperson. Suddenly the category is geographical and ethnic. As someone has said, this is like telling a story that features a priest, a deacon, and a Frenchman.[14]

More jarring still, the figure is an enemy. The animosity between Samaritans and Jews was extreme. Samaritans, descendants of alien people who mixed with the remnants of Israel's northern tribes, had obstructed the rebuilding of the Jerusalem temple (Ezra 4:2-5; Neh 2:19; 4:2-14) and aided the Syrians in their wars against the Jews in the second century B.C.E. Early in the first century C.E., Samaritans desecrated the Jerusalem temple at Passover with human bones.[15] Luke introduced Samaritans only forty-three verses earlier, reporting that when Jesus came to one of their villages, they turned him away (9:52-53). They had reason for their hatred. The Jewish high priest in 128 B.C.E. had burned the Samaritan temple on Mount Gerizim to the ground. It was said that eating with a Samaritan was like eating swine. If a Samaritan brought an offering to the Jerusalem temple, it was to be rejected.[16] Most telling for our parable, some rabbis declared that accepting aid from a Samaritan delayed the redemption of Israel.[17]

The situation, then, is this: if you are the victim in the ditch, the one approaching you now is the last person on earth you want touching you. You would resist him if you could, but you can't since you are too broken to move.

Like the priest and the Levite, the Samaritan "saw him." But his way of seeing is different from theirs. We are told that he "came near him" and saw him. There is a bit of suspense built into the narrative here. We see the Samaritan's close approach before we know what he will do. Not until the final word of verse 33 do we learn, "he was moved with pity." This is the only word of anyone's internal motivation in the parable.

What follows is noticeably elaborate. All we really need to know is that the Samaritan cared for the victim, but the story gives him no less than twelve verbs of care: "he was moved with pity ... went ... bandaged ... having poured ... put him ... brought him ... took care of him ... took out two denarii ... gave them ... said ... Take care of him ... I will repay." Here is an instance of that vivid extravagance so typical in Jesus' parables. In this case it may serve more than one purpose. It certainly conveys the stunning abundance of love's initiatives. The spate of verbs gives the sense that compassion is a steady, generous consistency of deeds.

The Samaritan attends to all present needs (medicines, bandaging, transport to a safer place, care through the night), but his compassion embraces the *future* as well.[18] His words to the innkeeper are the only dialogue in the parable, a directive for ongoing care and a promise to return and pay "whatever more." His compassion, present and future, is costly. He expends his supplies, money, and time. He risks his life on a hostile road, and he risks a blank check on an innkeeper (the trade was notoriously dishonest).

The catalog of verbs may serve another purpose. Jesus will soon ask, "Which of these three, do you think, was a neighbor?" We might resist granting the role to a sworn enemy. So, as Crossan says, "before the question can be put, the hearer must see, feel, and hear the goodness of the Samaritan.... The function of 10:34-35 ... is so to involve the hearer in the activity that the objection is stifled at birth."[19]

THE FRAME STORY CONCLUDED (VV. 36-37)

Abruptly, we are pulled out of the parable on the hook of Jesus' question, which permits no answer but one, "Which of these three, do you think, was a neighbor?" The lawyer cannot bring himself to say, "The Samaritan," but answers obliquely: "The one doing [*poiēsas*] mercy with him." Jesus answers like an echo, lobbing back the verb: "Go, and you do [*su poiei*] the same." We recall that their initial exchange was framed by this verb: "What must I do to inherit eternal life?" "Do this, and you will live."

If this seems like a simple conclusion, it is not. Radical shifts have occurred. Most notable is a shift in what "neighbor" means. At the outset it meant the *object* of love: "love your neighbor/who is my neighbor?"[20] Jesus, revolutionizing the word, makes "neighbor" the *subject* of love. The search for the right recipient of our care is subverted. We can no longer go looking for neighbors; "neighbor" now means us—provided we "go and *do* likewise." But how can we? The figure Jesus commands us to emulate is repugnant to us. We cannot identify with him. In fact, the parable left us no one with whom to identify except the wounded one, a dying man who would resist his rescuer if he could, but is in no position to have any say.

The parable, an apparent reply to a question posed from a position of control, hurls us into a position of no control. We are set down into a horrid place of life-and-death need, spurned by the upright who find us abhorrent, then shocked by our enemy's extravagant kindness. Here the parable abandons us. Having stripped us of all patronizing questions about our love, it leaves us in a ditch to know our need for *any* neighbor; and it leaves us at an inn—healing, paid for, and compelled to go and do, in uncalculated ways, what the unlikeliest compassion has lavished on us.

HOMILETICAL REFLECTIONS

This parable is often preached as a straightforward "example story." Luke may well understand it that way. Since his Gentile readers did not despise Samaritans, the shocking reversals discussed above were likely lost on them. "Go and do likewise," for Luke and many preachers since, can serve as the uncomplicated moral of the story.

David Buttrick, who fully appreciates the complexity of the parable, suggests that since white American mainline Christians do not see themselves as victims, the parable should probably be preached for them as a straightforward call to compassion.[21] Perhaps the most famous example of this approach did not rise from a white context; "On Being a Good Neighbor" by Martin Luther King, Jr., is still worth reading.[22] A variant of the "example story" approach, stressing that the Samaritan is an outcast, urges listeners to let their own painful experience flow into compassion for others.[23]

My conviction is that the text can be preached as the complex parable it is, along the lines offered in the interpretation above. The sermon will follow the text, scene by scene. Explanations of pertinent first-century realities must be made, but should be brief, lively, and bridged to current analogies. In various ways, we can establish identification with the wounded traveler. Our point of view on the three other travelers can be his; for example, "Here comes a priest."

True to the text, we need not dwell on the failure of the priest and the Levite. They are not villains, but foils. The Samaritan's arrival must evoke the proper shock. Beyond telling what must be told about Samaritans and Jews, we should help listeners to imagine this third figure as a type they fear or dislike. Who is this bearing down on our helpless position—if we are black? if we are liberals? conservatives? Americans? Whom do we fear, or would not want touching us? Whoever this is, it's someone we would avoid if we could, but we can't because we're dying, too broken to choose whose help we need.

Swiftly, we would show the details of the stranger's meticulous, intimate care, and just as swiftly exit the story as Jesus turns to us, glares, and asks who we think the neighbor is. The concluding minutes may reflect on where this leaves us—as people in no position to pick our neighbors, as people already touched by unlikely love and compelled to pass on the extravagant surprise of mercy.

Which brings us near to the issue of allegory. Since Jülicher, we've all had a good laugh at how the church for nineteen hundred years made allegories of the parables—and they outdid themselves with this one.[24] At the center of most allegories of this parable is the equation: Samaritan = Christ, who bears us out of death, heals our wounds, pays for us, and will return.[25] But Jesus surely didn't tell the parable as a code story about himself, so we won't preach it that way.

But this being clear, may we not also say that among the many trajectories of potential meaning spun out by this parable, some do, in fact, finally touch upon the story of God in Christ? We need not shrink from this. The sermon may point to it. This isn't allegory, but *witness* to a final mystery.[26] We have been joined in the ditches where we were dying by One we did not choose, borne out on terrifying arms that we might have resisted but cannot, covered in costly compassion that we cannot repay. In short, we live now by the mercy of a Samaritan God and a Samaritan Christ. The parable is not *about* these figures. But they move behind it and beyond it, and are the final source of our freedom to "go and do" unbounded compassion. The sermon can say so.

CHAPTER FIVE

A Man Entrusted His Money

For it is as if a man, going on a journey, summoned his slaves and entrusted his property to them; to one he gave five talents, to another two, to another one, to each according to his ability. Then he went away. The one who had received the five talents went off at once and traded with them, and made five more talents. In the same way, the one who had the two talents made two more talents. But the one who had received the one talent went off and dug a hole in the ground and hid his master's money. After a long time the master of those slaves came and settled accounts with them. Then the one who had received the five talents came forward, bringing five more talents, saying, "Master, you handed over to me five talents; see, I have made five more talents." His master said to him, "Well done, good and trustworthy slave; you have been trustworthy in a few things, I will put you in charge of many things; enter into the joy of your master." And the one with the two talents also came forward, saying, "Master, you handed over to me two talents; see, I have made two more talents." His master said to him, "Well done, good and trustworthy slave; you have been trustworthy in a few things, I will put you in charge of many things; enter into the joy of your master." Then the one who had received the one talent also came forward, saying, "Master, I knew that you were a harsh man, reaping where you did not sow, and gathering where you did not scatter seed; so I was afraid, and I went and hid your talent in the ground. Here you have what is yours." But his master replied, "You wicked and lazy slave! You knew, did you, that I reap where I did not sow, and gather where I did not scatter? Then you ought to have invested my money with the bankers, and on my return I would have received what was my own with interest. So take the talent from him, and give it to the one with the ten talents. For to all those who have, more will be given, and they will have an abundance; but from those who have nothing, even what they have will be taken away. As for this worthless slave, throw him into the outer darkness, where there will be weeping and gnashing of teeth." (Matt 25:14-30)

Jesus was a champion of the least advantaged. The Gospels report his advocacy and care for the left out, the pushed down, the little: children, women, the poor, the sick, the designated sinners. This commitment finds expression in his parables, which often give a celebrated role to an outcast or despised figure—a tax collector, a Samaritan, a widow denied justice, a failed son, inhabitants of "highways and hedges," a dead beggar.

The parable before us constitutes a singular exception. Here it is the one with the least who loses. We are shown three slaves holding varying sums of money. In stories using "the rule of three," we expect the third character, especially if disadvantaged, to turn out best; but here the last, the least, is excoriated and thrown into "outer darkness." This seems a bit like picking on Cinderella! The extreme judgment levied against this slave, especially since he commits no apparent wrong, shocks us into puzzled reflection.

AN ALTERNATE VERSION AND A QUESTION FOR PREACHING

The observations just made of the parable of the talents do not apply to its "parallel" in Luke 19:12-27, often called the parable of the pounds. Luke's version features a nobleman who, departing to receive a kingdom, entrusts money to ten slaves, each of whom gets the same amount (a *mina*, far less than a talent). One slave hides his *mina* in a napkin. On the nobleman's return, the profitable slaves are awarded cities. The slave who hid his money is rebuked and loses it to another, but is not punished. Luke's parable also includes some bloody business between the nobleman and an uprising of citizens on his return.[1]

The fact that Matthew and Luke present different versions of the same basic plot underscores a major interpretive issue. The Gospel parables are not verbatim reproductions of Jesus' parables.[2] Like other Jesus material, the parables were told and retold by early Christian teachers and preachers; inevitably, various modifications and versions evolved. The Evangelists not only drew from the traditions available to them but also exercised their own freedom in matters of context, vocabulary, style, and theological emphasis. As we shall see, the parable of the talents is replete with the special vocabulary, style, and theological interests of Matthew. Equally, the parable of the pounds reflects the style and purposes of Luke.

So when preaching a parable containing material more likely attributable to an Evangelist or his sources than to Jesus, what, exactly, does one endeavor to preach? Do we preach fully from the Gospel account, even if we feel certain that the parable of Jesus was somewhat different? Or do we discard some of the Gospel material, attempting something closer to what Jesus may have intended, though no such "original" is available to us? The first option may risk irresponsible naiveté; the second may risk irresponsible subjectivity and worse. Is there a kind of middle path? The parable of the talents provides a good case study for such questions.

THE CONTEXT

In more ways than one, Matthew's use of parables is forceful. First, most of his parables end in a downfall. Except for the brief narrative analogies of the treasure, the pearl, and the fishnet (13:44-50), *all* of the parables unique to Matthew are of this type, each of them ending on a note of judgment.[3] This pattern is consistent with Matthew's pervasive polemic against the opponents of Jesus, and his sober stress on the necessity of a new righteousness. Reading Matthew, we soon learn that a parable will likely end with a person or group condemned for being foolish or wicked.

Second, Matthew's parables often feature strong dramatic heightening. As John Donahue says, "Matthew loves the grand scale."[4] An apocalyptic sensibility contributes to this tendency; characters receive cosmic-sized recompense, as in our parable. More than this, it may be that Matthew as storyteller simply prefers more dramatic details. The currency described in our parable is massively bigger than in Luke's version. We have already observed, however, that Jesus' parabolic style brims with extravagant developments and details. If Matthew engages in "heightening," he follows a trajectory begun by Jesus.

Finally, we may observe that Matthew makes strong strategic use of the parables by placing them at points of major transition and emphatic conclusion. Matthew presents five great discourses. The central of these, chapter 13, is made entirely of parables, and functions as a "hinge" for the whole Gospel, depicting a turn from Israel to the disciples.[5] The first discourse, the Sermon on the Mount, ends in a parable of judgment that shows the crashing collapse of a house built on sand (7:24-27). The last discourse, entirely eschatological and delivered from the Mount of Olives (24:1–25:46), concludes with a thunderous cascade of no less than four parables of judgment. Our parable is the next to last of these.

As the third parable in the sequence, it is also the last of a distinctive triad of parables, each of which has the following in common: a powerful figure who makes himself absent; two contrasting courses of action taken in his absence; the arrival of the powerful figure; his positive response to the one(s) who did well; and his judgment on the one(s) who did not. The first parable (24:45-51) is about *slaves* whose *master* is *delayed*. The second (25:1-13) concerns *bridesmaids* when a *bridegroom* is *delayed*. Our parable tells of *slaves* whose *master* went *on a journey* for *a long time*. The first parable contains no surprise since the punished slave got drunk and beat the other slaves. But the next two parables feature five bridesmaids and a slave condemned not for acting badly but for failing to act. They receive withering rebuke and punishment for a kind of passiveness. It is a measure of the shock of this premise, and of its importance, that after confronting us with it in one parable, the Matthean Christ repeats it in another.[6]

HEARING THE PARABLE

This parable, like several others, involves slaves. "Slave," not "servant," is the meaning of the Greek word *doulos*. Slavery was prominent in the ancient Mediterranean world, including Palestine, where Jewish slaves served Jewish masters. Slavery in that culture differed from historically recent slavery systems like those practiced in America. It was not racially based, and the slaves were regarded as full persons. They were often educated, owned property, and held high-ranking professions. Still, they were subject to the will or whim of their master, and could receive harsh corporal punishment. The three men featured in our parable are not laborers but "managerial slaves."[7] Jesus' audience would have been familiar with the type—skilled and trusted with significant responsibility. That these three should be given charge of their master's property would come as no surprise.

The amounts of money given, however, are surprising. These are staggering sums. A talent (*talanton*) equaled about 6,000 denarii. If one denarius was the daily pay for a common laborer, and if a year included about 300 workdays, then 6,000 denarii—or one talent—equaled 20 years' worth of wages. Five talents represented 100 years' worth of wages. We are shown a man with his bags packed, hugely rich, flinging great fortunes into the hands of slaves.

The amounts are decidedly uneven. While the nobleman in Luke's parable parcels out smaller amounts[8] in equal measure (19:13), the man who gives talents not only entrusts giant amounts but does so asymmetrically: five, two, and one, "each according to his ability." Many scholars take this phrase as a bit of Matthew's didactic allegorizing, but it seems consistent with the characterization of the master. In both the extravagance and the asymmetry of his disbursements, he is radically *free*. The varied amounts suggest that he has not been aloof from the slaves. They are not all the same to him. He knows them right well. The word for "ability" here is *dynamis*, often translated "power." What this man especially knows in them—and trusts—is their power.

He gives them not one word of instruction. Commentators regularly state that everyone—slaves and hearers of the parable—knew that the money was given in expectation of trade and profit, but the silence of the text remains. Luke's version observes no such silence; the nobleman gives the blunt order, "Do business with these until I come back" (19:13). The man who gives talents gives no order. As the slaves are trusted with vast sums, they are trusted also to discern their course of action. They will do so unsupervised. The parable's first scene is a flurry of disbursements, followed by an abrupt departure. Like so many of Jesus' parables, this one unfolds under the arc of a monumental absence.

One slave begins "immediately." He is off like a shot, trading (*ērgasato*, literally, "he worked") with the five talents and gaining five more. The second slave's work is more briefly sketched: "Likewise the one with two gained two more."[9] Again, we are in a story shaped by "the rule of three," moving swiftly to the third character, who will do something different.

He digs a hole and buries the fortune. It is not an odd choice. In that era the practice was common. Jesus told another parable that featured such a stash (Matt 13:44). Rabbinic law prescribed the burial of money as the best security against theft,[10] and Josephus described how, after destroying Jerusalem, the Romans recovered much of the city's wealth from where its owners had buried it in the ground.[11] The narrative makes no comment on the third slave's motives. We simply see him doing what people in that culture did to safeguard a treasure.

Having depicted two ways of handling the master's money, the parable now narrates his return. "After a long time," he "came and settled accounts" (v. 19). The latter verb *(sunairō)* occurs only twice in the New Testament, both times in parables about slaves in Matthew. The first of these (18:23-34) describes a king who "wished to settle accounts with his slaves" and began with one who owed—impossibly—ten thousand talents. It is not yet clear what is "owed" in our parable.

The first two slaves report their successes in identical fashion. Both "came forward" speaking the same lines, "Master, you handed over to me five/two talents; see, I have gained five/two more talents" (vv. 20, 22). A comparison with Luke's version reveals that Matthew's account once more gives a greater sense of the slaves' autonomy. In Luke the first two slaves say, "Your pound has gained" (19:16, 18), while in Matthew they say, "I have gained."

In his response the master is, once more, extravagant. These are his first lines, spoken twice, identically to both slaves: "Well done, good and trustworthy slave; you have been trustworthy in a few things, I will put you in charge of many things; enter into the joy of your master." This is decidedly *not* how we expect a master to speak to slaves. Jesus, in fact, told another parable whose whole premise is that slaves are never thanked or invited to sit at the master's table, nor should they expect to be (Luke 17:7-10). This master not only heaps praise on his slaves, but he also promises to increase their responsibility and invites them to "enter into the joy of your master." The last line, exuberant and mysterious, has a startling ring of eschatological glory.[12]

The third slave now comes forward. His speech is three times longer than that of the others (thirty Greek words to ten). While the first two begin by recalling the master's gift, "Master, you gave ...," the third starts by declaring his perception: "Master, I knew...." He then utters three clauses of accusation. The first indicts the master's character: you are "a harsh man." The next two indict the master's actions: "reaping where you did not sow, and gathering where you did not scatter seed." He matches the accusations with three verbs for himself: literally, "and fearing, going away, I hid your talent in the ground." Then, abruptly, this: "Look, you have what's yours!"

Like the affirmations poured on the first two, the master's response to the third slave is shockingly extreme. He calls him "wicked and lazy" and "worthless." In midspeech he stops addressing him, as if already the slave has ceased to be present, and tells others of his fate, ordering him thrown into "the outer darkness, where there will be weeping and gnashing of teeth."[13] Any doubt about whether we are still in the "real world" is swept away. The ground of the story heaves open to the Abyss.

Before disposing of the slave, the master questions him: "You knew, did you, that I reap where I did not sow, and gather where I did not scatter?" This taunting echo of the slave's words notably omits his summary of the master's character; the word *harsh* has been dismissed. The next line, about investing the money with bankers, functions not to tell the slave what he should have done, but to show that he acted inconsistently with what he says he knew.[14] A real conviction that the master is greedy would prompt at least a minor investment. The slave's honesty is in question, as is his opinion of the master. This seems especially true in view of what the master now does with the talent that the slave has tried to return. Instead of taking it, he gives it to the first slave. Throughout the story he has done nothing but give. He gives great sums to slaves. He gives them huge praise, gives them higher responsibility, gives them astonishing entry into a master's joy. No mention is made of his taking the profits. Now, insulted and told to take back his money, he doesn't, but gives even that away.

So the parable offers two opposing perspectives on the master: one described by the third slave, and the other implied in the actions of the first two slaves and of the master. In the light of the latter, it is clear that the third slave has seen the master falsely. His problem is called elsewhere in this Gospel an "evil eye" (6:23); he sees only darkness, which fills him with darkness and, in the end, swallows him in "outer darkness."[15] The master he "knew" for a ruthless tyrant is, in fact, hugely trusting and grandly giving.[16]

The first two slaves seem to know this. They are unafraid to risk the money. Refusing safety, they play the great game of growing the gift. Surely, this carries a risk of failure, a possible loss of the master's money. Maybe they don't fear a loss because they don't fear a generous master. Maybe they can even guess his response to a risk that ends in failure: "Well done! You've been faithful in a little—I will give you more."

The ultimate violation of such freeing generosity is to feel it as mean; to regard the trust as a threat, to collapse gracious immensities to the paltry size of one's own projections. To do so means living as if one is not gifted, to rail against unfairness while an entrusted fortune lies untouched in the backyard.

The parable is a stark instance of where Jesus repeatedly locates the fiercest judgments of God. The ugliest sin is refusal to act on divine goodness. The church's age-old penchant for distorting this point is nicely illustrated in an alternative version of this parable included in the apocryphal *Gospel of the Nazarenes*. In that version, the slave who buries the master's money receives only a rebuke; punishment is reserved for another slave, who spent the master's money on "harlots and flute players"![17] The point of that story is that the worst we can do is to be worldly; Jesus' point seems to be that the worst we can do is nothing.

HOMILETICAL REFLECTIONS

This parable, like so many others, presents us with the challenge of cultural details that do not easily translate into contemporary terms: masters, managerial slaves, the talent, the burial of cash. The challenge is to honor the original sense of such details *and* to bridge them into contemporary terms *and* to do so as seamlessly as possible. How do we speak, for instance, about the talent itself? An excursus on its value strains the sermon, and given the great difference in economies, coming up with an exact equivalent for our culture is impossible.[18] My advice is not to belabor it. A talent is a boatload of money—that's what we need to know. Round it up at half a million bucks, which gives the approximate sense. And be mindful that this word is not a play on the English term for special aptitudes or abilities. That definition of *talent* was actually derived from how this parable was preached. Jesus' story deals in cash.

The parable's effect requires our identification with the third slave. The first hearers probably identified with his action and with his view of the master.[19] Instead of moralizing about his choice, it is best to locate ourselves in it. The faithless choice of individuals—and churches—to opt for self-protection, holding the gifts of God in timid reserve, is hardly rare. Having named our own anxious misapprehensions of God and of the trusts we are given, we may reorient the listeners to a wildly generous God and to our startling freedom to take glad and faithful risks with all we have.[20]

Earlier we raised the question of how much to preach those elements of a parable that belong more to the Evangelist than to Jesus. We are well advised, I believe, to take a Gospel's version of a parable quite seriously, generally including those elements that may well rise from the Evangelist's interests and style. Discernment is called for, however, in how much *weight* to assign these elements; and our decisions in this regard will at least partly depend on our best sense of what is true to the intention and manner of Jesus.

For example, what if Matthew, as some scholars claim, upgraded the currency in the parable from a more modest sum (like Luke's *minas*) to the walloping talents, consistent with his love of "the grand scale"? For at least two reasons, we do well not only to follow Matthew but also to stress the magnitude of the sum. In the first place, the shocking size of what is entrusted seems key to the characterization of the master. In the second place, whether or not "talents" is original to Jesus, we know that extravagant detail typifies his manner of proclamation, notably in the parables. So the sermon marvels at a master who gives each slave a *fortune*.

Most of the other "Matthean" details here may be treated similarly. "Enter into the joy of your master" and "throw him into the outer darkness, where there will be weeping and gnashing of teeth" may be Matthew's eschatological heightening of the story; but they are consistent with the shock often present in Jesus' parables and prompt us rightly to consider the ultimate immeasurable consequence of our choices.

When it comes to Matthew's narrower eschatological use of the parable, however, there is reason for pause. In context it seems clear that Matthew sees the master's return as an allegory for the parousia of Christ. Jesus likely told the parable as a metaphor of responses to the generosity of God. We would be wise to focus on the latter. This should not be a sermon about the Second Coming. Nor, it should be added, is the parable a warrant for asserting that death will take us to a God who demands, "What did you do with what I gave you?"—the very Master construed by the third slave. The parable proclaims joyous freedom under great grace. Still, we cannot neglect the story's undeniable thrust toward the future and a final judgment on human life. As we speak of what it means to live with a fortune in our hands, we may rightly cast an eye to the ending that will take us all, and to the hope that eternity rings with God's gladness over all who took the trustful risk.

CHAPTER SIX

A Rich Man Clothed in Purple

There was a rich man who was dressed in purple and fine linen and who feasted sumptuously every day. And at his gate lay a poor man named Lazarus, covered with sores, who longed to satisfy his hunger with what fell from the rich man's table; even the dogs would come and lick his sores. The poor man died and was carried away by the angels to be with Abraham. The rich man also died and was buried. In Hades, where he was being tormented, he looked up and saw Abraham far away with Lazarus by his side. He called out, "Father Abraham, have mercy on me, and send Lazarus to dip the tip of his finger in water and cool my tongue; for I am in agony in these flames." But Abraham said, "Child, remember that during your lifetime you received your good things, and Lazarus in like manner evil things; but now he is comforted here, and you are in agony. Besides all this, between you and us a great chasm has been fixed, so that those who might want to pass from here to you cannot do so, and no one can cross from there to us." He said, "Then, father, I beg you to send him to my father's house—for I have five brothers—that he may warn them, so that they will not also come into this place of torment." Abraham replied, "They have Moses and the prophets; they should listen to them." He said, "No, father Abraham; but if someone goes to them from the dead, they will repent." He said to him, "If they do not listen to Moses and the prophets, neither will they be convinced even if someone rises from the dead." (Luke 16:19-31)

The parable of the rich man and Lazarus is so haunting and so fiercely direct that, before attempting an in-depth analysis, we would do well simply to stand before it, to absorb what we can, and to say what we see. Arriving at the Grand Canyon, we don't want a geologist at our elbow explaining the strata. We want to gaze for a while, to trace the colors, the scope, the depth for ourselves, to pay attention to what is before us and what it stirs within us. Such a practice is always a fitting first approach to a sacred text. Before reaching for lexicons and commentaries, we notice what we notice.

OBSERVABLE PATTERNS

1. This parable evokes the *senses* to an unusual degree, at extreme points of both pleasure and pain. *Pleasure*: for the eyes, gorgeous purple; for the skin, the feel of fine linen; for ears, nostrils, and palate, all the delights of merry feasting; more ethereally, a lifting strength of angel arms, the warmth of Abraham's bosom, the cool waters of paradise. *Pain*: rank hunger, the ache of bones on pavement, deep sting of skin ulcers, dogs nosing the sores, the gall of public exposure and neglect; and elsewhere, agony in flames, a cry of thirst, a cry for mercy. We are starkly confronted with bodies, with the comforts a body may crave and the suffering a body may or may not endure.

2. The story is a dense grid of *contrasts*. Attributes of each man have counterparts in the other: one is rich, the other poor; one feasts daily, the other goes hungry; one is covered in purple and linen, the other in sores. Some contrasts are achieved by pointed silences: the story names one man Lazarus but utters no name for the other; it notes a burial for one but is silent on the disposition of the other corpse; it describes angels carrying one of them but says nothing of attendants to the other man's soul. Contrasts also appear in the verbs given to the two: Lazarus has no active verbs except that he longs for food and dies. He is only acted upon: he is left by someone at the rich man's gate[1]; sores cover him; dogs abuse him; angels carry him; Abraham comforts and defends him. He never says a word, nor is he spoken to. The rich man speaks *about* him, suggesting he be sent on errands; Abraham speaks *for* him. The rich man, on the other hand, is a whirl of active verbs and has plenty to say, at least in death.

3. *Reversals* abound. Reversals are contrasts *imposed*, and the ones imposed here are massive. The man formerly draped in luxuriance

is now wrapped about by flames. His once-sated appetite is reduced to craving a water drop on a fingertip. The man he'd ignored is the man he now cries for. Having refused a beggar, he is now a beggar refused. For Lazarus all reversals are happy. The slobbering dogs are replaced by a convoy of angels. The erstwhile nobody sprawled in a gutter, starving within the sound of elegant dining, is not only transported to paradise, but he holds there the highest place of honor, seated beside Abraham himself at the final feast. These reversals are embedded even in the syntax. Twice describing their lives on earth, the story tells of the rich man first and Lazarus last (vv. 19-21, 25a); twice describing their lot after death, Lazarus comes first, the rich man last (vv. 22, 25b). Perhaps we can note one other odd reversal: a gate seems to have become a chasm.

4. Finally, we notice the *shape* of the story. More than one pattern of structure is discernable. Based on setting, we have a two-part story with the first scene (vv. 19-21) set on earth and the second (vv. 22-31) in the afterlife. Based on narrative mode, a different two-part sequence is evident, one part description (vv. 19-23) and the other a dialogue (vv. 24-31). Perhaps we should see the parable as set out in three movements: (1) the two men in life—verses 19-21; (2) the great reversal after death—verses 22-24; and (3) the dialogue—verses 25-31. The dialogue is apparently crucial, since it takes up well over half the parable. Its last two exchanges concern the rich man's brothers and Abraham's insistence that they hear "Moses and the prophets." Thus, the conclusion returns our attention to the living and points adamantly (and surprisingly?) to the Scriptures.

HEARING THE PARABLE

The original audience would have heard echoes and nuances in this parable that we do not. Folktales about reversals after death were well known at the time. Such a tale from Egypt, possibly carried by Alexandrian Jews to Palestine, may lie behind similar Jewish stories preserved in the rabbinic literature. One of these features a rich tax collector and a poor scholar.[2] The tax collector dies and is given a great funeral, while the scholar's burial is unattended. A colleague of the scholar sees in a dream that his friend now resides in a beautiful garden "watered by flowing streams," and the publican leans over a river with his tongue stretched out, unable to reach the water. Scholars have suggested that Jesus borrowed from the common stock of such folktales, and that his hearers would have found aspects of the scenario familiar.[3] If this was the case, then elements of the parable not matching the folktales may bear particular significance.

One striking feature of the parable is that, unlike its popular counterparts, it makes no mention of piety or righteousness or sins committed. We are simply shown two men in proximity to each other, one wealthy and the other destitute. Never does the story refer to the rich man as impious or ungodly. In fact, as we shall see, he was likely regarded by the audience (and himself) as a righteous and pious man. All that we are shown of him in the opening tableau is the pleasures that his wealth affords him, which are impressive. The "purple" he wears is reserved for royalty and elite officials. In the Roman Empire there were rules about who could wear purple and how much they could wear.[4] Linen, the most highly prized of exported fabrics, was his undergarment. Sumptuous feasting was associated with special occasions, but remarkably, he "feasted sumptuously every day." Nothing else is said of him.

Nor is anything said of the character of Lazarus. Some commentators suppose him to be pious, based on his place in the afterlife and on the meaning of his name.[5] "Lazarus" is a Greek form of the Hebrew name "Eleazar" or "Eliezer," meaning "God helps." But the name is no warrant for ascribing any merit to the man. The name does exercise a powerful function in the story. On one level it has an initial ironic force—a destitute man starving to death named "God-Helps"! The name points to his social isolation; as no one else helps him, he is abandoned to the help of God. And in the retrospect of the parable's ending, the name turns out to have been a kept promise. Perhaps most important is the fact that he has a name at all, a feature found in no other parable of Jesus. Lazarus's neighbors ignore him to death, but the parable knows his name, counterasserting his personhood. The rich man has everything else; Lazarus has a name. The church's tradition of correcting this asymmetry by naming the rich man Dives (Latin for "rich") violates part of the parable's point.

The misery of Lazarus gets more than twice the description accorded the rich man's pleasure. The misery matters more. The first detail locates him at the very gate of conspicuous consumption. The verb used for his "lying" there implies that he was unable to move himself (see n. 1). Further, a horrid skin disease covers him in sores. Next named is his hunger. The expression behind "longed to satisfy his hunger" employs a verb that refers more often to animals than people.[6] The Greek suggests "a constant and unfulfilled longing," implying that he got nothing.[7] The focus of his hunger, "what fell from the rich man's table," was likely the bread used by guests for wiping their hands. The harassment by dogs, lapping at the fluids in the sores of a man too weak to fend them off, is a final grisly insult. Why are we told of this? Mention of the sores and the dogs does not advance the plot. Such details confront the hearers with vivid horror, inviting us to revulsion at the extremity of a human being's misery.

He dies and is carried by angels to the bosom of Abraham, which is probably a reference to feasting in the realm of God. As the Beloved Disciple is said to have been in the bosom of Jesus at table (John 13:23), so Lazarus now enjoys a place of intimacy and honor beside Abraham at the heavenly banquet. By contrast, the rich man died "and was buried." Typically in such stories, much is made of the quality of funeral given for the unrighteous one. Many interpreters comment on the importance of burial in that culture, on the lavish proceedings implied for the rich man, and on the likelihood that Lazarus is denied any such honor; but the parable's silence on this matter is impressive. In fact, after describing the extravagant compensations granted to Lazarus, the terse remark "and was buried" almost certainly implies a contrasting void.[8]

Hades is the Greek word used to translate the Hebrew term *sheol*, the realm of all the dead. By the first century the idea had evolved in some circles that the unrighteous were separated from the righteous in this realm, where final judgment was awaited. But the parable is not offering a topography or timetable of the afterlife. It draws from folklore to make a larger point. Still, the spatial arrangements in the parable are striking. In his torment, "he lifted up his eyes" (RSV). Apparently, he is in the lower position now. He must look up to see Abraham "far away" and Lazarus in his bosom.

The question must now be raised: would the audience of the parable have been surprised and disturbed by what they had heard so far? There is good reason to suspect that they were. Though stories of reversal in the afterlife were common, the determining factor was always which characters were righteous and pious, and which ones were not. The parable refuses those categories. When we recall the widely held belief, backed by certain sacred texts, that righteousness was rewarded with prosperity and sin was punished with penury and disease (see below), we begin to realize that Jesus, once again, may have set up his hearers for a shock.

Now the dialogue begins. The man (he is no longer called rich) addresses the patriarch as "Father Abraham," implying a claim of kinship. He sees himself as a child of the promise. Even as he cries for mercy, his sense of entitlement permits him to employ imperatives. "Send Lazarus," he says. He knows the name of his starving neighbor after all, yet even now he misses the man's value. He sees Lazarus not as celebrated guest but as Abraham's servant and his own.[9] "Have mercy, send Lazarus," is a terribly ironic cry. The man he would not serve is the one he wants to be served by now.

Abraham's reply first acknowledges kinship—"Child"—then offers an imperative of his own: "remember." The call to remember pertains solely to what the arrangements used to be: "during your lifetime you received your good things, and Lazarus in like manner evil things." That is all. Then he adds, as if the inevitability of reversal were perfectly obvious: "now he is comforted here, and you are in agony." There is also the matter of the chasm: "between you and us a great chasm has been fixed . . . and no one can cross." "You" is plural; others occupy the thirsty side of the abyss. The chasm itself is apparently a surprise; nothing like it appears in ancient literature on the afterlife.

Having been refused, the man changes his tack: "Then, father, I beg you to send him to my father's house—for I have five brothers—that he may warn them, so that they will not also come into this place of torment." It is sometimes said that this line signals a dawning human concern in the man, but more likely the plea for his family is to be heard as another expression of elitism. No remorse is expressed, no concern for the likes of Lazarus, only a sense of threat to his peers.[10] The substance of the request, incidentally, is not that Lazarus be raised from the dead. The intent is for a "spirit" (Luke 24:37 RSV) or "angel" (Acts 12:15) of the deceased to make an apparitional visitation.

Abraham's answer is curt: "They have Moses and the prophets; they should hear them." (English cannot convey the force of the second clause, a third-person imperative.) "Moses and the prophets" is a reference to the texts of the Torah and the Prophets. Most Jews of the day accepted the Prophets with the Torah as constituting Scripture. The retort means something like: They've got the Bible; let them read it! The call to *hear*, however, is more potent, since in Jewish thought, "hear" *(shema)* means "Hear and obey."

Having been twice denied, the man's final speech is argumentative: "No, father Abraham; but if someone goes to them from the dead, they will repent." He is suddenly a theologian. From Hades he plies father Abraham with religious vocabulary; his last word (in Greek as in English) is *repent*. He is claiming expertise. He knows what it takes to reach people of his class. It takes special treatment, "insider information."[11] The Bible, so domestically familiar, could hardly shock the wealthy into change.

Besides, the pious rich were already reading the Bible—certain portions, at least—and finding great assurances there. Deuteronomy 28, for example, promises prosperity of all kinds as God's reward for obedience and guarantees every possible impoverishment and calamity (skin ulcers included) as the sure result of disobedience. Psalm 1 specifies of the righteous, "In all that they do, they prosper," and then declares, "The wicked are not so." As we have lately been reminded, there is the highly profitable prayer of Jabez (1 Chron 4:10). Most pointedly, there is the case of Abraham himself, famously rich because God favors him (Gen 13:2; 24:35). Such texts prop up the view that wealth and health equal reward/blessing, while poverty and disease equal punishment/curse. So in Jesus' day it was widely held that one's personal fortunes were willed by God and deserved. Such a construal may lie behind the insistence of the man in Hades that the Scriptures will not change the minds of his brothers.[12] Stressing certain texts has deafened them to the heart and the voice of the text as a whole. They are sufficiently inoculated against the affront of Scripture. Only a jolt will do, as from Lazarus's ghost.

Father Abraham will have none of it. He closes the conversation and rings down the curtain on the parable with this: "If they do not listen to Moses and the prophets, neither will they be convinced even if someone rises from the dead." This final declaration ups the ante. The ex-rich man has argued for an apparition to save his brothers; Abraham says if they won't heed Moses and the prophets, not even a *resurrection* can help them.[13] With a Bible in your hand and a beggar at your gate, if you cannot see what must be done, the ultimate miracle is wasted on you.

CONTEXTUAL CONFIRMATIONS

The parable's setting in Luke may sharpen our sense of it. At first glance, Luke 16 seems disjointed. A parable about a crooked manager (vv. 1-8a) gives way to a jumble of sayings, ending with: "You cannot serve God and wealth" (v.13c). Luke says the Pharisees, "who were lovers of money," responded with ridicule (v. 14). Jesus accuses them of justifying themselves and prizing what is an abomination to God (v. 15). The topic then shifts to "the law and the prophets," which he declares inviolable (vv. 16-17), a claim supported in his pronouncement against divorce (v. 18). Our parable, which follows, reflects both issues addressed in the verses preceding it. Like verses 14-15, the parable's first part confronts the love of wealth; like verses 16-18, the parable's conclusion confronts the disregard of Scripture.[14] As the parable makes clear, the two issues must be seen as one. Scripture forbids the prizing of wealth and insists on equity for the poor.[15] Recipients of Scripture who live otherwise deafen themselves to the One who breathes not only in the texts but also in the sufferings of those for whom the texts plead. The voice of God sighs from the Scriptures and from the poor; to shut out either is to shut out both.

The parable relates to other passages in Luke. It enacts the reversals proclaimed in Mary's song (1:52-53) and in the blessings and woes pronounced by Jesus (6:20-26). It echoes John the Baptist's dismissal of those who call Abraham "father" and do not bear the fruits of repentance (3:8), and anticipates Zacchaeus, another rich man, who festively repents by giving half his· wealth to the poor and making reparation for unjust gain at 300 percent interest, whereupon Jesus confers on him the title "son of Abraham" (19:8-9). In a strange way the parable may also resound in the Emmaus story (24:13-35). A risen man joins two travelers, who grasp neither his message nor his identity. He refers them to "Moses and all the prophets" (v. 27), and still they cannot comprehend him. But when they extend hospitality and a meal to the stranger, comprehension comes. Words from a resurrected man quoting Moses and the prophets leave them unpersuaded until, sharing supper with him, they know him in the breaking of the bread.[16]

HOMILETICAL REFLECTIONS

Since the parable joins the themes of justice and Scripture, our preaching of it may do the same. On this point, the lectionary (C, Proper 21 [26]) is generous. Amos 6:1a, 4-7, the Old Testament option complementing the Gospel, is an exact instance of what the five brothers must hear. The epistle reading, 1 Timothy 6:6-19, confirms that the economic concerns of Moses and the prophets are shared ringingly by the church.

With whom would the parable have its hearers identify? The story leaves little option. Neither the rich man nor Lazarus, being dead, is available. The only characters left alive are the five brothers, in whose position the story finally abandons us, to pursue justice and mercy for the poor as Scripture requires, or face divine judgment.

Preachers should not theologize their way around this. Jesus makes his one theologizing character a resident of hell. The story's teller unmistakably voids the option of rescue by one who is raised from the dead if we refuse the prior grace of the plain law to love our neighbor.

Neither does the text warrant assaulting the listeners with accusation and our best attempts at prophetic rage. We are preaching a parable, a form whose effectiveness lies precisely in its refusal to lecture or harangue. Notice how the form works here. Instead of spelling out what to do or how to feel, the parable holds up strange pictures that create taut disturbances. We are shown stark inequities and stunning reversals, then pointed to Scripture as sufficient light by which to make our way. Father Abraham, voicing a lean exposition of what the parable knows, speaks his lines with disarming calm. His restraint does not lessen the pathos and urgency of the story but gives them room to enlarge in the listener. Preachers may wisely take their cue from him.[17]

Finally, in preaching such a text we should resist a kind of simplification that is both dishonest and unhelpful. An industrial world like ours creates and sustains poverty in more complex systemic ways than did the agrarian world of Jesus and his hearers. Mammoth realities of class stratification, undergirded and exacerbated by governments, corporations, and societies, have made Lazarus legion. The new Lazarus is not much helped by isolated divestments. Astute listeners know this. For the parable to do its contemporary work, we should acknowledge the vastness of the chasm that gapes between poor and nonpoor, pointing to possibilities of repentance that, without neglecting faithful individual self-giving, include commitments to far-reaching structural change.[18] This need not be said heavy-handedly; a few brief lines can suggest the scope and tangle of our problem. Individual listeners, preachers included, are not left off the hook for personal repentance. The often-noted widening "gap" between rich and poor in the world constitutes a chasm, according to the parable, that is dangerous, now or later, to all of us. Crossing to the life-giving side begins at our own gate, by what we bring out and who we invite in. Moses and the prophets make this clear, as confirmed by the One who rises from the dead.

CHAPTER SEVEN

Someone Sowed Good Seed

The kingdom of heaven may be compared to someone who sowed good seed in his field; but while everybody was asleep, an enemy came and sowed weeds among the wheat, and then went away. So when the plants came up and bore grain, then the weeds appeared as well. And the slaves of the householder came and said to him, "Master, did you not sow good seed in your field? Where, then, did these weeds come from?" He answered, "An enemy has done this." The slaves said to him, "Then do you want us to go and gather them?" But he replied, "No; for in gathering the weeds you would uproot the wheat along with them. Let both of them grow together until the harvest; and at harvest time I will tell the reapers, Collect the weeds first and bind them in bundles to be burned, but gather the wheat into my barn." (Matt 13:24-30)

Books on the parables often neglect the parable of the planted weeds. Studies focused on selected parables usually pass over it, and at least one volume offered as a full commentary on the parables of Jesus gives no reading of it, the author being confident that Jesus said nothing like it.[1] I include it here because others omit it and because it rewards consideration. It offers a particularly useful case study of how multiple meanings and applications can coil in a single parable. One interpretation of it—allegorical, apocalyptic, and ascribed to Jesus—is given by Matthew (13:36-43); but other interpretations are plausible, more compelling, even insistent. The longer one ponders this parable, the wider and deeper its reach.

A PARABLE OF JESUS?

The Jesus Seminar judges this parable as not likely from Jesus, on the grounds that it "reflects the concern of a young Christian community to define itself over against an evil world, a concern not characteristic of Jesus."[2] Scott, who helped write that opinion, frames his reason for rejecting the parable in slightly different terms. He states that it reflects the primitive church's struggle over whether to expel members considered evil. Since the concern for marking community boundaries was not part of Jesus' agenda, Scott attributes the parable to the church.[3] Thus, two related objections are raised: the parable is said to reflect anxiety about the church in the midst of an evil *world* and anxiety about evil *in the church's ranks*, and Jesus had neither anxiety.

It is fair to say that both anxieties are evident in Matthew. His own interpretation of the parable designates the impure field as "the world" (13:38), and the apocalyptic tilt of his Gospel leans constantly toward a cosmic purging. On the other hand, Matthew demonstrates a special concern with impurity inside the church itself (see 7:21-27; 13:47-50; 22:11-14), another stubbornly weedy field. The twin concerns to which the parable may be addressed in Matthew, however, need not define its meaning for Jesus, who may have told such a story precisely as counterpoint to someone else's anxiety.

The quest for purity was fervently and variously practiced among contemporaries of Jesus in Palestine. Revolutionaries (Zealots) dreamed of purifying Israel of Roman occupation through violent uprising. The Essenes, dismayed not only by intruding pagans but also by a corrupt temple establishment and a fouled populace, withdrew to the desert to be an isolated community of radical purity. Most effective was the purification movement of the Pharisees. Embracing careful observance of Torah, buttressed by a complex of Torah-protective oral law, with special attention to acts of devotion and purification, the Pharisees kept a fire of brilliantly separated holiness within an occupied and compromised land. Such commitments required strict distance from those who did not share them, but at issue was Israel's identity, the survival of a heritage and a vital faith. How else to preserve this heritage and faith against so many blatant and subtle incursions of pagan rot and domestic drift? The need was for holiness, and holiness meant rigorous, keen-eyed separateness. There was no lack of insistence on it in the Scriptures.

Enter Jesus. He does not come preaching separation but is characterized by scandalous inclusions. Notoriously, he dines with prostitutes, imperial collaborationists, and their ilk. He points clearly to Torah and speaks unmistakably of repentance but seems liberal on Sabbath law, is loose on purity ritual, and admits all manner of uncleanness into his company. When criticized for such poor boundaries, he counters that his critics are boundary-obsessed, that their separations do harm. So while some in Israel want purity by ousting enemies, he teaches the love of enemies. While others seek purity by withdrawing from society, he inhabits all manner of cities, dwellings, and institutions. While still others seek purity by devoutly observing religious duties, rituals, and bans, he enjoys rough company and breaks small laws with an odd nonchalance.

Any number of people may have been vexed by Jesus' tolerance of the mixed state of things around him. Some, especially Pharisees, would have found his seedier associates a rank contradiction of the claim that God's reign was dawning in his work.[4] But some of his disciples may have been just as perplexed by his inclusions and his silences,[5] as would be anyone else who dreamed of an Israel or a world cleansed of corruption. Why is he so nonresistant to evil, so silent on purity, so at ease with ambiguity, so surrounded by questionable characters? Any such question might have gotten from him a story about an unanxious farmer whose earnest servants, eager to rip weeds from wheat, are told to mind their own business and leave a mixed field alone until other hands in other times can do the rightful sorting. God's domain is like that, he would have said; and they would have walked off, shaking their heads.

Such a parable, then, could well have come from Jesus. The fact that a version of it appears in the *Gospel of Thomas* may strengthen the case.[6] The precise shape of the underlying original parable is, of course, uncertain.[7]

Context and Interpretation in Matthew

Matthew 13:1-53, the third of five discourses of Jesus in this Gospel, is a bundle of eight parables, plus two parable interpretations and two statements on the purpose of parables. In Matthew's larger plot, something decisive is happening here. This flurry of parabolic material signals a great shift in the work of Jesus as presented by this Gospel. Matthew 11–12 narrates a storm of tensions and conflicts with Jesus, and the beginnings of plots to kill him; so now in 13:1-53 he speaks of oppositions, rejections, and failures, and turns the focus of his ministry from the masses to the disciples.[8]

Matthew sees parables as the perfect mode of speech for making such a pivot. When the disciples ask Jesus why he speaks to the people in parables, he says "the secrets of the kingdom" are being disclosed to disciples and kept hidden from the crowds (v. 11). Parables here are Jesus' way of giving more understanding to those who already have some, and further baffling those who have none (v. 12). This divide is dramatized twice when Jesus privately "explains" parables to the disciples (vv. 18-23, 34-43). In fact, the very moment that constitutes the "seam" of Matthew's Gospel, turning his ministry from the crowd and toward the disciples, occurs precisely as he enters a house (13:36) to give a private elaboration of our parable.

The parable of the weeds is thematically linked to other parables in the discourse. It is the second of an opening triad of seed parables, each of which features a planting followed by a surprise. In the parable of the sower (13:3-9) the surprise involves multiple losses of seed but still a good crop. Our parable, too, bears the surprise of a threatened crop that will still come to harvest. The parable of the mustard seed (13:31-32) hangs on the double surprise of a tiny seed yielding a substantial plant, which, even so, is weedlike and hardly the majestic tree that prophets had used as metaphor for a kingdom truly equipped to house "the birds of the air" (that is, the nations, see Ezek 17:22-23; 31:2-6; Dan 4:10-12). All three seed parables, in other words, include a note of scandal or strangely mixed results. There is a mixing as well in two of the remaining parables. Yeast, considered unclean, is hidden by a woman in a big batch of flour (13:33), and a net filled with fish has nasty ones flopping among the good ones (13:47-48). Though all of these parables do not make the same point, they share images of unwanted elements, the mixing of "good" with "bad," and the perception of threat.

Matthew has a keen interest in clarifying the final disposition of all threats. The interpretation he reports of the parable of the weeds is focused on that theme. This interpretation (13:36-43), placed on the lips of Jesus, is clearly Matthew's composition. In the first place, these verses are packed with language and concepts found only in Matthew. Jeremias counted in these eight verses no fewer than thirty-seven instances of linguistic usage peculiar to Matthew.[9] But more than this, while the parable itself centers on a farmer commanding his slaves to let the weeds grow, 13:36-43 seems mostly to be a warning against being a weed. Three verses (13:40-42) are given to detailing their destruction, while the farmer's patient call to forbearance is ignored.[10]

What we have in 13:36-43 is not an interpretation of the parable but Matthew's addendum, in severe apocalyptic terms, on the fate of "all causes of sin and all evildoers" (13:41). Verses 37-39 assign referents to the characters and certain components of the parable—seven instances of this-equals-that—but such a fixed, allegorical list is out of sync with the characteristic parabolic method of Jesus, whose stories are most often richly textured, expansive, blooming into profusions of meaning and application.[11] On its own terms, the parable of the weeds turns out to be such a story.

HEARING THE PARABLE

The parable divides into two parts: a narrative that describes two sowings (vv. 24-26) and a dialogue between the owner of the field and his slaves (vv. 27-30). Since the interaction between master and slaves is twice as long as the initial narrative, the parable's center of gravity is in its second part.

Jesus likens the kingdom of heaven "to someone [*anthrōpō*] who sowed good seed in his field." Calling the seed "good" would seem unnecessary, but what happens next will prompt the slaves to this very question: "Did you not sow good seed?" We recall that the foundational biblical story of beginnings also stresses that it was "very good."

But not all sowing is good. There is an enemy who comes at night, sowing terrible seed. This counterplanting, too, occurs inside Jesus' likening of the kingdom. The kingdom is like someone sowing good seed *and* an enemy sowing seeds of poison, helter-skelter, on top of them. Just as the parable allows weeds to stand with wheat, the kingdom includes an enemy presence busily at work in the dark.

That the sabotage occurs at night, "while everybody was asleep," marks the enemy's work as surreptitious, and it suggests that the operations of evil, its massive insinuations of itself among the good, are matters of impenetrable mystery. Who or what is this enemy? Where did it come from? How did it get in? Why, and to what end? The answers, if any, are wrapped in thick shadow. The parable locates it all beyond our observing, in the night, as we slept. Nor can this sleeping be construed as a failure to be properly watchful. The farmer, too, was sleeping.

Earlier in this book, we met another parabolic farmer who slept after scattering seed (Mark 4:26-29). Many scholars have thought that Matthew, having that parable before him, created the parable of the weeds as a variation of it. After all, he is following much of the sequence of Mark 4, and the parable of the weeds falls in exactly the place of the other parable and shares some of its vocabulary. The two parables, however, have substantially different plots and themes, and each in its own right has a good claim to be authentically from Jesus. Assuming this is so, Jesus told two parables about farmers who are notable for a distinctive absence of anxiety.

One would think that the farmer in our parable has reason to be anxious. What the enemy sowed in the farmer's field is not just any weed. *Zizania* (meaning "cheat") is *lolium temulentum*, also known as darnel. It commonly grows in fields of wheat, which it closely resembles until maturity. Its roots are strong and can uproot the wheat. Worse, it is poisonous. If its seeds are ground together with the wheat, the result is inedible and potentially deadly. Little wonder that its name is "cheat."

Though darnel is a common problem in the Middle East, the scenario described here is surreal. Someone deliberately plants a field full of it, an act of vandalism made all the more absurd if we imagine the perpetrator meticulously collecting all these weed seeds.[12]

The result is unheard of—not the common problem of some weeds in the wheat, but prodigious numbers of them, a full crop of them thoroughly commingled with and competing against an original crop now under assault.

Understandably, the slaves are alarmed. Enough time has elapsed for the crisis to be evident. What they bring to the "householder" (*oikodespotēs*, master of the house) are three questions. First, "Master [*Kyrie*], did you not sow good seed in your field?" As indicated by the grammar of the question and the lack of pause for an answer, they know full well that the seed was good; but the mess in the field makes their asking irrepressible. The second question then tumbles on top of the first: "Where, then, did these weeds come from?" More urgent to them than the question of *what to do* in this catastrophe is the question of *how and why* it has come. It is a good question, faithful to the need of human beings under assault for an accounting. Their master doesn't give them much. "An enemy has done this" is all that he says, and the darker mysteries remain.

So now the third question: "Then do you want us to go and gather them?" "No," says the master. It is an emphatic and startling response. Good farmers and gardeners wage war on weeds. The slaves assume it and are asking for the order. As noted above, darnel can uproot wheat, and "harvesting" both together can risk ruining the good grain. A few recorded cases exist of Palestinian farmers leaving darnel alone, but the general practice is to weed it out, and to do so repeatedly.[13] With such a massive and threatening infestation, why let lethal weeds grow rampant?

The farmer gives his reason: "in gathering the weeds you would uproot the wheat along with them." Two factors may underlie his verdict. First, darnel and wheat are look-alikes. Though enough growth has occurred that weeds are evident, the slaves may still mistake some of the wheat for darnel. Far worse, given such a huge infestation, the roots of the plants are all intertwined.[14] Pulling the weeds may rip out the wheat. Leaving the weeds alone is a risk to the crop, but this farmer locates the unthinkable risk in trying to separate what is, for now, inseparable.

This is his command: "Let both of them grow together until the harvest." Separating is for another time. To underscore his point, he says "harvest" twice, three times really, since the Greek words for "harvest" and "reapers" are *therismos* and *theristai*. Let them grow until *harvest*, and at *harvest* time I will tell the *harvesters*. This last word makes clear that not only does separating belong to another time, it belongs to other hands. So the slaves are not even granted a role in the final discernment between wheat and weeds.[15] In fact, this field seems managed entirely without them. The farmer, not they, sowed the seed. The reapers, not they, will harvest. The slaves ask for one job, but it is refused. They work for the farmer, belong to him, but the management of this field is all his.

"I will tell the reapers, Collect the weeds first and bind them in bundles to be burned." Though fire is a standard biblical metaphor for judgment, Jesus may have another surprising turn of plot in mind. Wood for burning is scarce in Palestine, so weeds are dried, compressed, and burned for fuel. This constitutes a kind of final joke on the enemy, whose intended sabotage is put to good use,[16] perhaps even for the baking of some quite delicious wheat bread.[17]

HOMILETICAL REFLECTIONS

Since the parable is so much richer than the allegorical grid laid over it, we should stick to the story. The lectionary couples the parable with the allegory, but a sermon that takes its cues from the allegory forfeits most of what the parable says and seeks to do. Still, some allusions to the allegory may serve. A painting by the English artist Roger Wagner shows a vast sunlit field of wheat being harvested by angels, beautifully working scythes and tying sheaves. No weeds are evident. Two paths intersect in the field, suggesting a cross, a shape repeated in the shadows of angels' wings.[18] This eloquent image, drawn from the allegory and transcending it, has a fitting, provocative place on a theological trajectory arcing from the parable itself.

A point of entry for the sermon is not hard to find. The parable begins by raising large, perennially relevant questions. How did everything get to be such a mess? Everywhere we look, evil insinuates itself into the good. The world and every person, institution, and community in it are compromised and threatened by evil encroachments. The preacher can articulate the awful fact of it and the pained question posed in the parable: Why is this so? The parable does not answer the question, and neither may we. But the story's opening images suggest this much, theologically and pastorally: the compromised state of things is a given; it opposes divine intention; its origins are hidden in mystery. The image of an enemy in the night is aptly ominous and opaque; it is an image that keeps many silences.

The sermon will then address our unwise inclinations to attack what we judge to be evil. The purity impulse is the dominant religious and political reflex of every age and notably our own. It is a rage to isolate, separate, and destroy what we hate or fear. It is an impulse to do violence. It underlies all purges, persecutions, schisms, scapegoating, and war. When this impulse is not employed in active forms of violence, it does other damage, breeding dishonest blame and dumb fantasies of what the world could be, what the church could be, what we could be, if only we were rid of *them* or *that*.

Jesus forbids it all. We are not competent, he says, to discern. What we judge to be evil may bear more good than we know, may serve in the end a vital purpose. Even if our judgments are correct, charging into mixed fields with machetes and weed-whackers does inevitable harm. Good and evil are now inseparable, snarled at the roots; violence against evil invariably is violence against good.[19] So just at the point where we presume to know what is evil and place ourselves above it to destroy it, we become evil.

It is important to notice where we locate ourselves in the parable. Primarily, of course, our position is represented by the slaves. But we naturally see ourselves also as the farmer's good planting. How sobering to realize that *all* who read this parable assume they are the wheat. It is not a safe assumption. A sly feature of the story is that no one knows which is which. The One who alone can discern may know our lives, our churches, our nation, for weeds, soaking up the resources of a rich field and yielding no fruit, posing as the good but, in fact, hindering its growth.

Scholars have often said that the point of the parable is a call to be patient. This may be true, but perhaps it is more pointedly a warning against naiveté. Jesus confronts our easy presumption that we know what is evil, even in ourselves, or that we can excise it. It is also naive, of course, to think we can do nothing about evil. The parable cannot be construed as a call to passiveness, and perhaps the sermon should say so. We can resist further sowing of evil seed, do some creative counterplanting, see to our own repentance, and actively love our enemies. Nothing passive about any of that.

In the end, the parable moves beyond all of this to invite us toward amazement. Our impure fields are accepted and redeemed. One thinks of the old paintings of Christ in Gethsemane, a garden always infested with thorns. They show him kneeling among them—at night while others sleep. In the morning, he will wear the intruding thorns as his crown. He is a sign of the Owner of all gardens and fields, who abides ambiguities, blesses contradictions, and turns thorny ground to holy ground. The final harvest of such grace will at the last be lifted into light like the bread of Eucharist. Until then, we trust, we praise, we grow toward the One who loves the impure field.

CHAPTER EIGHT

A Rich Man Had a Manager

There was a rich man who had a manager, and charges were brought to him that this man was squandering his property. So he summoned him and said to him, "What is this that I hear about you? Give me an accounting of your management, because you cannot be my manager any longer." Then the manager said to himself, "What will I do, now that my master is taking the position away from me? I am not strong enough to dig, and I am ashamed to beg. I have decided what to do so that, when I am dismissed as manager, people may welcome me into their homes." So, summoning his master's debtors one by one, he asked the first, "How much do you owe my master?" He answered, "A hundred jugs of olive oil." He said to him, "Take your bill, sit down quickly, and make it fifty." Then he asked another, "And how much do you owe?" He replied, "A hundred containers of wheat." He said to him, "Take your bill and make it eighty." And his master commended the dishonest manager because he had acted shrewdly. (Luke 16:1-8a)

A large lake of ink has been drained by scholars writing on this parable. It's the kind of text that is dear to the heart of an academic: difficult, obscure, bristling with interpretive uncertainties begging for a theory—and theories abound. For precisely these reasons, ordinary folk in the church, most preachers included, are less enamored of it. Our problem is not just the oddly amoral ending of the story: a boss praising a terminated manager who has apparently just ripped him off. At a more basic level, it is simply hard to know what happens in the story. Maybe the first listeners understood it perfectly, but we could use more information. What socioeconomic matrix connects "debtors," "steward," and "master"? Is the master a decent fellow or a greedy tycoon? How, exactly, is the steward "unjust"? What really happens in the debt reductions, and at whose expense? Assuming we could answer such questions, we are still left to wonder: what could possibly be the point for us?

CONTEXT AND PARAMETERS IN LUKE

Any assessment of this parable must consider not only what precedes it in Luke but also what comes after, and in particular must ask, where, in this case, does "after" begin? There is a very old uncertainty about where the parable ends. Luke 16:8a says, "And the master praised the unjust steward because he had acted shrewdly." "Master" in Greek is *kyrios,* and a possible meaning of the line is that Jesus, the Lord, having finished the parable, praised the steward. The parable, then, would end at verse 7 with the slashing of debts. This view assumes that a boss's praise of his steward's fraud is unlikely.[1] Most interpreters believe that verse 8a does refer to the steward's boss, twice called "master" earlier in the parable (vv. 3, 5). The plot seems to want a concluding response, which turns out to be, as so often in the parables, surprising.

The saying in 8b, "for the children of this age are more shrewd in dealing with their own generation than are the children of light," was probably attached to the parable before it came to Luke. Verses 9-13, a collection of sayings on "mammon," are placed here as Luke's attempt to shed further light on the parable. Notably, they are not entirely consistent with each other, as if to say, "The parable could mean this, but it could also mean that, but on the other hand. . . ."[2]

Oddly enough, the richest clues to the parable's meaning in Luke may lie not in the sayings that follow it but in the story preceding it. The parable of the unjust steward follows, in more ways than one, the parable of the father who had two sons (15:11-32). The modern chapter divisions in our Bibles, convenient as they are, can create artificial divisions. Imagine you are reading Luke without the dividers of numbered chapters and verses. You read a story that begins, "A certain man" *(anthrōpos tis)* had two sons. The younger son squandered *(dieskorpisen)* his father's living. Now in a life-threatening crisis, he speaks a soliloquy ending in a plan for survival. He acts on it. His father responds with startling joy; the plan is transcended. When this parable concludes, another begins in the very next sentence. "A certain man" *(anthrōpos tis)* had a steward accused of squandering *(diaskorpizōn)* his property. Now in a life-threatening crisis, the steward speaks a soliloquy ending in a plan for survival. He acts on it. His master responds with startling praise; the plan is transcended.

Now there is certainly more to each of these parables than this sketch shows, and the parable of the unjust steward is by no means a simple reiteration of the prodigal's story. But the echoes of vocabulary and plot are unmistakable. Luke seems to be inviting reflection on the parable of the steward as another case of a doomed squanderer who takes a prudent turn that is overwhelmed by impossible acclamation.[3]

SOCIOECONOMIC BACKGROUND AND SOME INTERPRETIVE THEORIES

Before working through the text, we should survey some of the many answers supplied by interpreters to questions about the parable's assumed world, the qualities of its characters, and the meaning of the actions undertaken in the plot. To make this discussion accessible, some simplification is necessary. Instead of attempting a short "history of interpretation," the discussion is organized around several questions.

1. What social and economic conditions underlie the story? In first-century Galilee, land was being consolidated into large estates held by wealthy individuals and families. Peasant farmers were dispossessed of their lands. The estates were subdivided and leased out to tenants, who paid substantial rents and interest. Since the economic disparities were stark and farming is always chancy, life was precarious for all but the landowning elite. These dynamics constitute the real-world context for the story.

2. Who are the debtors, and what do they owe? The assumption of most scholars is that they are tenants; but some have suggested that they might be merchants who owe for goods received.[4] How could merchants owe oil and wheat, instead of cash, to the estate?

In a much-quoted article, J. D. Derrett[5] pointed out that though Jewish law prohibits usury, a common way of subverting the law was to convert cash loans into loans for "equivalent" commodities, inflating them greatly and effectively hiding usury. Similarly, the "rents" owed by tenant farmers were inflated. How high was the markup? Standard interest on monetary loans was 25 percent. For produce the rates were much higher, with added interest rates (insurance) based on the commodity's vulnerability. The debts owed in this parable are steep (the oil of about 150 olive trees, the wheat yield of 100 acres, roughly worth 1,000 and 2,500 denarii, respectively).[6] The debtors are either farmers working big tracts or merchants doing big business. That they can read and write (vv. 6-7) is an added indication of relative stature.

3. *What are we to think of the master?* Since rich landowners commonly charged exorbitant interest against their debtors, the first hearers of the parable would almost certainly have assumed that this master was usurious, and therefore impious and wicked. Nothing in the parable contradicts this. But some interpreters go further, claiming that everything he does in the parable is reprehensible. They state that the charges against the steward are false, that the master arbitrarily sides with the accusers, refusing him a chance to defend himself.[7] The praise he gives the steward for reducing the debtors' load is mixed with malicious delight, it is said, because now that they owe him gratitude, he can gouge them in new ways.[8] Such readings of the parable go well beyond what the text can support.

4. *What is the steward's role, and what has he done in the parable?* The job of a steward (*oikonomos*) was to supervise the financial affairs of the estate. As agents of the landowners, who often lived elsewhere, stewards wielded considerable power, writing and enforcing contracts, overseeing all aspects of the business. Some stewards were slaves, but this one is an employee, a retainer; otherwise instead of dismissal he would have gotten a beating and a demotion, maybe worse. Stewards were well known for engaging in graft of their own. It was expected that they would add commissions to be paid by merchants and tenants; the master wouldn't mind, provided his profits were ample. The charges brought against this steward must allege something more serious. Commentators have made various guesses: embezzlement, laziness, taking too much commission,

and so on. As already noted, some interpreters declare him innocent.

Theories of what he did by reducing the debts include the following: (1) he removed the master's usurious take; (2) he cancelled only his own cut; (3) he simply reduced the master's income to buy favor with the debtors; (4) he got even with his hateful ex-boss; or (5) having earlier brought shame to his boss in the eyes of the community, he restored the master's honor in the sight of all.[9]

5. So the parable is doing what? More options: it (1) tells us to make faithful use of money; (2) warns us, in the crisis of the kingdom, to act boldly for our salvation; (3) offers the comedy of a rogue's escape, inviting us beyond our own "dead seriousness"; (4) forces us to reconsider what justice is; (5) invites us to a vision of all debts forgiven; (6) presents the steward as a Christ figure scandalously forgiving debts; or (7) is an angry depiction of those who practice economic injustice.[10] There are still other verdicts, but what shall be our own?

Hearing the Parable

The story divides into four scenes. Scene 1: The boss has words with the manager. Scene 2: The manager has words with himself. Scene 3: The manager does business with the debtors. Scene 4: The boss has words for the manager.

Scene 1 (vv. 1-2). The rich man has heard "charges" against his manager. So the parable starts with trouble, and the source of it is ambiguous. Some interpreters assert that the accusers are "backstabbing" merchants or tenants who are circulating "anonymous slander or gossip" in a kind of power play against both the manager and the master,[11] but it is best to let the reticence of the text stand. The verb for the bringing of charges is *diaballō* (the word *diabolos*, devil, is its kin), which means to accuse with hostile intent, either falsely or justly. The verb tells us only that the charges have a punitive outcome in mind. The content of the charges is also ambiguous. "Squandering" the owner's property suggests anything from embezzlement to wasteful spending to incompetence. We have already noted that the same word in the previous chapter names the prodigality of a younger son.

We learn of the charges before the manager does. He is now "summoned" (v. 2). "What is this that I hear about you?" says the boss. He is not looking for an answer; the matter is decided. His command is literally, "Give back the word [*logon*, in this case, "account"] of your stewardship." Its most likely meaning is: turn in the books. We need not infer an audit. He is being fired and must turn in his records for his successor's use. The termination is then made official: "because you cannot be my manager any longer."

The man makes no response. His silence, too, is ambiguous. Is it an imposed silence? a guilty silence? a stunned silence? a grimly accepting silence, guilty or not, of the massive, incontestable power that has doomed him? Is it the silence of the drowning, struggling mutely for life? We do not know. At the very least, this is the silence of someone covered in accusation and great loss, a silence that most human beings come to know.

Scene 2 (vv. 3-4). Outside the master's presence, the man speaks to himself. As happens elsewhere in parables from Luke (cf. 12:17-19; 15:17-19; 18:4-5; 20:13), we overhear the secret wrestlings of a character with a problem. "What will I do?" As in scene 1, this conversation begins with a "what" question. He ponders two intolerable options: "I am not strong enough to dig, and I am ashamed to beg." How are we to hear these words? The tendency is to hear them comically—a little fellow in a jam, telling himself he can't possibly be dirtied with manual labor or face the indignities of panhandling—like something from a fat, funny servant in a comic opera.

But hearing him in this way doesn't fit the story.[12] He has wielded tremendous power, has served the elite, is educated for valued skills. He is no buffoon. And what he rejects is a good deal worse than "panhandling" or just any manual labor. "Digging" probably refers to work in the quarries or mines, not usually survived. Even digging in orchards or fields was grueling work, done by peasants who were long toughened by it and against whom he could not compete. Begging was worse—utter disgrace, malnourishment, early death. An *oikonomos* contemplating digging or begging shows the desperation of his plight. He is homeless. He lacks the skills for which his world might offer employment. The skills he has will not be wanted from him, given his disgrace. His master has thrown him into outer darkness.

"I know what I will do," he says. He has hit on a plan that might save him yet. If it works, "people may welcome me into their homes." Is he aiming at a way to become a circulating houseguest of a new set of friends? Or is he hoping for new employment in the kind of work he knows? We do not know, but the latter seems more likely. He doesn't say what his plan is, of course. We get to watch it unfold.

Scene 3 (vv. 5-7). He calls in the rich man's debtors, meeting with them one at a time. The story narrates two of the interviews. "How much do you owe my master?" he asks the first. He had also said "my master" in his soliloquy, but using it here keeps the debtor unaware of the new situation. If the debtor does know, he isn't talking.

To ask what is owed is unnecessary—he holds the bill—but this is how business is done. "A hundred jugs of olive oil" is the reply, about 900 gallons, exceeding the value of what a laborer could earn in three years. "Take your bill, sit down quickly, and make it [*grapson*, write] fifty." A 50 percent cut! We don't have to be told that he took it. Of special interest is that he is to write the change "quickly." It is a marker, apparently important, that the manager is moving swiftly. No time to waste, he acts with dispatch.

So he speaks to the next man more tersely, just four Greek words: "And you, how much do you owe?" "A hundred containers of wheat." The exact volume is uncertain, but 1,000 bushels is a fair guess, worth two and a half times more than the first man's oil. "Take your bill and make it eighty." A 20 percent cut, but apparently, the same cash value given the first man, 500 denarii.

We may return now to the prior question of *what* is cut in these debt reductions. The amounts really seem too high to represent even a rapacious manager's "commission," and there is reason to believe that whatever graft he was up to would be under the table, not in the books. Is he, then, removing the owner's usurious interest? Some have argued that the figures match the typically exorbitant interest applied to these commodities, but it remains a matter of dispute. Even if the numbers match, would Jesus' hearers, or Luke's readers, know the rates? While usury is to be assumed in a rich landowner of the time, all we may really know is that the manager has made substantial reductions of his boss's income. And he has done it apparently by acting as if still representing him.

Whether the debtors saw through the ruse is an open question. We are left to wonder if winks were exchanged as the contracts were redrawn. But he summoned them like an agent of the owner, and did business with them, as always, as if it were so.

Scene 4 (v. 8a). The master has found out. Maybe he has just now read it in the documents, handed over as commanded by the manager. Or maybe he heard it first from someone else, having asked what the raucous party in town was about. But he knows now, knows that what everybody owes him has been cut 20 percent here and 50 percent there and who knows how much else. And he knows it was done by someone acting like his agent after being told he was fired.

And he *praises* him. "Commended" is a fair translation, but given the surprise of the commendation, why not give the word *(epaineō)* its full voice. Another word also wants its full voice here. *Adikia* means "unrighteous," "unjust," "wicked." "He *praised* the *wicked* manager" honors the tension in the line. His wickedness is not fully disclosed—ambiguity again. We heard accusations, maybe true, of squandering his employer's property; then we saw him acting as his agent when he wasn't, cutting unauthorized deals, giving away funds of the man who fired him, and doing so to buy future favors for himself. The parable calls him wicked.

He is praised because "he had acted shrewdly." How so? By making his master appear generous? By causing a riot of joy that the owner is in no position to stop?[13] By creating a win/win/win situation—reduced payments for debtors, restored reputation and honor for the boss, and the same for himself? By turning, for a while at least, from making money to making friends?[14] All of these, perhaps, and more. Does he get a new job? Get back his old one? Who knows? All we hear is a master's strange praise of a wicked manager who has acted shrewdly.

That last word *(phronimōs)* appears in other parables and sayings of Jesus: another manager called "faithful and shrewd" (Luke 12:42; Matt 24:45), five shrewd bridesmaids (Matt 25:2, 4, 8, 9), and a shrewd man who built his house on rock (Matt 7:24). The disciples are to be shrewd as snakes (Matt 10:16). Also translated "wise," *phronimōs* is wisdom with a sharp eye on the future, and pointedly pragmatic. Pragmatic action is highlighted semantically in the parable. The manager's first line is, "What will I *do*?"

(poiēsō). On reflection he says, "I know what I will *do*" *(poiēsō).* The very last word of the parable is the same. The master praised him because—*phronimōs epoiēsen*—"shrewdly he *did.*"

HOMILETICAL REFLECTIONS

A parable that leaves so much unsaid puts interpreters in the position of making choices. As evident from the discussion above, a bewildering variety of choices has been made about what kind of story the parable is telling and, consequently, the kind of response it might intend to evoke. Clearly, some decisions have to be made.

But supplying too many answers in the interest of solving a parable's ambiguities is, especially for the preacher, unwise. Granted, certain points of historical information must be supplied if the sermon is to be faithful, not to mention comprehensible. In the case of this parable, some judicious description of the social and economic relationships that inform the story is necessary. Care should be taken, however, against making claims for the plot that the parable does not support. The parables of Jesus are good fictions, and good fictions have reasons both for what they disclose and for what they withhold.

Ambiguities in a text may actually bear remarkably strong gifts for a listening congregation. If a preacher lifts up an ambiguity in a text and slowly turns it for the listeners, suggesting possibilities— Is it this? or this? or this?—the listeners are given room to connect where they connect.[15] For example, instead of claiming that the steward's silence means he is guilty or that it means he is falsely accused and given no recourse, we can hold out the options, as was done above: guilty silence, angry silence, helpless silence.... According to their own experience, listeners will quietly take their places in the story, as the parable may well intend. Having presented the possibilities and acknowledged what we cannot know, we can then state what *is* known: that this is the silence of someone covered in accusation and devastating loss, a silence that is painfully common, sooner or later, to us all.

Whatever open questions remain in the parable, this is the core of the story: a participant in a crooked system, pronounced guilty and facing catastrophe, takes quick, risky, unauthorized action to save himself. He does it in a crooked way—how else?—dispensing crooked cash, reducing debts, making friends. The aim of his flurry of action is his survival; what he receives is his master's praise.

It's a messy little story. It invites reflection on the messy systems we are part of, our own compromised and accused situation, our mixed motives and mixed means for acting redemptively. The use of money and property will come into it, the lightening of what others must pay, the making of grateful new friends by our highly imperfect and always self-interested generosities. The parable, in the end, is kind to us. It relieves our illusions of being good or of having to become good. It knows where we live and what we are and, remarkably, holds out gracious praise for the hopelessly wicked, like us, who will do what they must to be saved.

CHAPTER NINE

A Man Had Two Sons

There was a man who had two sons. The younger of them said to his father, "Father, give me the share of the property that will belong to me." So he divided his property between them. A few days later the younger son gathered all he had and traveled to a distant country, and there he squandered his property in dissolute living. When he had spent everything, a severe famine took place throughout that country, and he began to be in need. So he went and hired himself out to one of the citizens of that country, who sent him to his fields to feed the pigs. He would gladly have filled himself with the pods that the pigs were eating; and no one gave him anything. But when he came to himself he said, "How many of my father's hired hands have bread enough and to spare, but here I am dying of hunger! I will get up and go to my father, and I will say to him, 'Father, I have sinned against heaven and before you; I am no longer worthy to be called your son; treat me like one of your hired hands.'" So he set off and went to his father. But while he was still far off, his father saw him and was filled with compassion; he ran and put his arms around him and kissed him. Then the son said to him, "Father, I have sinned against heaven and before you; I am no longer worthy to be called your son." But the father said to his slaves, "Quickly, bring out a robe—the best one—and put it on him; put a ring on his finger and sandals on his feet. And get the fatted calf and kill it, and let us eat and celebrate; for this son of mine was dead and is alive again; he was lost and is found!" And they began to celebrate.

Now his elder son was in the field; and when he came and approached the house, he heard music and dancing. He called one of the slaves and asked what was going on. He replied, "Your brother has come, and your father has killed the fatted calf, because he has got him back safe and sound." Then he became angry and refused to go in. His father came out and began to plead with him. But he answered his father, "Listen! For all these years I have been working like a slave for you, and I have never disobeyed your command; yet you have never given me even a young goat so that I might celebrate with my friends. But when this son of yours came back, who has devoured your property with prostitutes, you killed the fatted calf for him!" Then the father said to him, "Son, you are always with me, and all that is mine is yours. But we had to celebrate and rejoice, because this brother of yours was dead and has come to life; he was lost and has been found." (Luke 15:11-32)

This best-loved of all the parables is emotionally the richest. To read or hear it thoughtfully is to be moved. The three main characters, vividly rendered, regard each other with extreme feeling, powerfully enacted and twice explicitly named (vv. 20, 28). Most impressively, our own emotional identification may well *shift* as the story proceeds. The father's pathos and soulful joy in welcoming the younger son easily move us; but then we meet the son who never left and, unless we have been biased by bad preaching, we cannot help identifying with his anger and hurt. The parable's genius is its capacity to create identification with each character, which means that we experience the story from conflicting perspectives. It is, in other words, as strangely inclusive and encompassing as the astonishing father it presents.

CONTEXT IN LUKE

We have already seen surprisingly close links between our parable and the one that immediately follows (16:1-8a), but more obvious ties are evident with the two that precede. The three parables of Luke 15 are presented as Jesus' response to the Pharisees and scribes, who "were grumbling and saying, 'This fellow welcomes sinners and eats with them'" (15:2). The parables of the lost sheep (15:4-6) and the lost coin (15:8-9) are twins. Each begins as a question: "Which one of you . . . ? / What woman . . . ?" Each describes a single thing that is lost from a group of others like it, which is searched for and found by the protagonist, who calls friends together to celebrate, saying, "Rejoice with me, for I have found [what was] lost." Each is followed by a tag line declaring great joy in heaven when a single sinner repents (vv. 7, 10).

Similarities in the parable of the father of two sons are obvious. A single member of a larger group (a family) disappears, and his reappearance results in a celebrative gathering. The language of lost and found is reiterated (vv. 24, 32), as is the language of rejoicing (v. 32). It may also be said that the center of each of the three parables is not the one who was lost but the one who reclaims and calls for celebration.[1]

But differences abound. Instead of a question, our parable delivers a long and complex narrative—complex because its whole cast is human. Sheep and coins do not willfully lose themselves, but a son does. Calling the neighbors in to rejoice over a lost coin or sheep may strike us as odd, but throwing a party over a reappeared stinker is closer to scandal. And, in fact, the father's response exceeds celebration; he showers his ruinous son with outright honors. In the context of Luke 15, then, our parable takes the situation of verse 2 seriously in a way that the first two parables do not, creating a scene of celebrating that really is objectionable. The plot is further complicated by the fact that the character who expresses the objection has objectionable qualities of his own. This begins to feel like real life. The human complication of the story is underscored by two final differences from the preceding parables of Luke 15: the conclusion of this narrative is left pointedly unresolved; and no tag line about joy in heaven follows, for the story leaves us in the shoes of one who cannot (yet?) concede joy.

HEARING THE PARABLE

The brief opening sentence lays out what might be called the geometry of the parable's relationships. The subject of the sentence, "a certain man," will remain the center of the story. Lines of relationship are drawn from him to the other two: he "had two sons." The verb belongs to him. The other two are not called brothers; no line of relationship connects them to each other. Whether they can become brothers is the unresolved question of the parable.

The story begins with an imperative issued by the younger son: "Father, give me the share of the property that will belong to me." He intends to leave home and wants his share of the inheritance now. As the younger of two sons, his share is probably one-third of the estate (Deut 21:17). Since a man's property was his until his death, the son's request is disrespectful, even scandalous. For all practical purposes, he is pronouncing his father dead.[2] Some scholars argue that the scandal does not lie so much in the request itself as in the son's liquidation of the property and squandering of it.[3] A family's property had to maintain its oldest members for life. Whatever a son may have received before his parents' deaths would have to be managed responsibly for their sakes. Either in demanding his inheritance or in dissipating it, most likely in both, the younger son commits a kind of patricide.

And the father, without a word, complies. He agrees to be dead. His action, by common standards, is foolish. Sirach 33:19-22 warns:

> To son or wife, to brother or friend,
> do not give power over yourself, as long as you live;
> and do not give your property to another,
> in case you change your mind and must ask for it.
> While you are still alive and have breath in you,
> do not let anyone take your place.
> For it is better that your children should ask from you
> than that you should look to the hands of your sons.
> Excel in all that you do;
> bring no stain upon your honor.
> At the time when you end the days of your life,
> in the hour of your death, distribute your inheritance.

A saying from the Babylonian Talmud decries any man "who transfers his property to his children in his lifetime" (b. B. Meṣi'a 75b). Not to be missed is the Greek word for what the father now divides between his two sons. The demand was for the "property" (ousias), but the father's compliance is stated in different terms: "he divided between them his living"—his life (bion).

Soon the son has "gathered all he had." The verb may refer to converting the property into cash,[4] possibly even selling land. He travels to "a distant country," that is, the Diaspora, a Gentile land.

What happens there is narrated swiftly, conveying the sense that his downward slide was precipitous: "and there he squandered his property in dissolute *[absōtōs]* living."[5] We are spared the details. We know only that "the prodigal" indulged in unprincipled, destructive ways till all he had was gone.

When he is down to nothing, famine strikes the land of his dreams. Scarcity swallows him. In desperation he indentures himself to "one of the citizens of that country," a wealthy Gentile, who assigns him to tending pigs. It is work no Jew should have, a final defilement of himself (Lev 11:7; Deut 14:8). His degradation becomes absolute when he finds himself craving pig food. The "pods" they ate were carob, the eating of which by humans is associated in rabbinic literature with the most wretched impoverishment.[6] Miserably, he longs to fill his belly with these, but "no one gave him anything." *No one* is emphatic.

At this we are told that "he came to himself." What does this mean? Consorting with swine and ogling their food, maybe he knows himself now for a pig. Some have asserted that coming to himself amounts to profound repentance, but the expression is surely more ambiguous.[7] At the very least it means that in a new way he realizes the desperation of his circumstances and that he must somehow act to change them. His mind flies homeward to his father's hired hands, who "have bread enough and to spare." His sober assessment of himself is, "I am dying," anticipating his father's double declaration: "he was dead" (vv. 24, 32). To save himself from dying, he says what he will do: "I will get up and go to my father, and I will say to him, 'Father, I have sinned against heaven and before you; I am no longer worthy to be called your son; treat me like one of your hired hands.' "

The speech is framed theologically; it is a confession declaring sin "against heaven," that is, God, and sin "before you," his father. Does he mean this? Perhaps he does. Still, we know him for a rascal—a rascal now starving and humiliated. Who can say what such a person in such a crisis might say, and why, to save himself? The parable, impressively, leaves the question open. Like most of us, his turning homeward may be mixed. Repentance is always, in any case, self-interested, its full implication dawning by degrees.

The part of his speech that declares, "I am no longer worthy to be called your son," is certainly true. He has effectively pronounced his father dead and delivered into the hands of foreigners what should have sustained his father's future. His filial duty is forfeit; he cannot function as son. His hope to become a "hired hand" *(misthios)* refers to the status of a day laborer, an unstable position, dependent on irregularly available work.[8] Having made his plan, he "got up," an enactment of the rising *(anastas)* he had proposed (v. 18). He begins the long walk home.

Abruptly, the story's perspective shifts. We now stand beside the father, who saw him "while he was still far off." Was he watching for his son's return? Like the Samaritan (10:33), seeing yields to being "filled with compassion" and moving toward the other. Shockingly, he breaks into a run. Mothers might run to their children; fathers did not. He must hike up his long robe, show his flying legs, and look foolish to all.[9] On reaching him, he "put his arms around him [literally, fell on his neck] and kissed him." This language echoes other biblical scenes of emotionally charged reunion (Gen 33:4; 45:14; 46:29). The verb for the kiss is an intensified form *(katephilēsen)*, conveying great passion. Again, he is oddly motherlike. And the whole unbridled display of acceptance occurs before a word has been spoken.

We should probably see this highly demonstrative welcome as, in part at least, an act of intervention. Members of the community would be hostile to the prodigal for his betrayal of the most basic moral values of the culture. Approaching his former home exposes the young man to cruel insults from onlookers, and perhaps worse. Running to him and publicly embracing and kissing him may well be an act of the father's protection.[10]

The son begins his speech, getting out his confession, but before he can ask to be a hired hand, he is cut short. The father's words are not even to him, the sprint and the rapturous embrace having said it all. His words are for others: "Quickly," he says, bring the best robe (his own?) and a ring (a signet ring, sign of authority) and sandals (slaves, not sons, go barefoot). And a feast is commanded—the prized fatted calf, no less—a considerable upgrade of the son's dream of "bread." "Let us eat and celebrate; for this son of mine was dead and is alive again; he was lost and is found!" These four gifts—robe, ring, sandals, and feast—are conferred to communicate the son's honored status not only to him but pointedly to the community itself. No one is to question his full sonship.

His father acts to assure no shaming of the son by anyone. He is to be honored by all. Since a calf feeds a great crowd, we are to imagine the whole village joining in the festive welcome of the son.

It feels like an ending, but it isn't. From the start we have known of two sons, and we must hear from the other. We meet him headed home from work. Coming in from the field, he hears the sounds of "music and dancing." A servant (*pais*, boy) explains: "Your brother has come." It is the parable's first use of the word *brother*. He adds that the fatted calf was slaughtered for the occasion. There is nothing subtle about the older son's response: "he became angry and refused to go in."

And why should he not be angry? His brother has betrayed the family and shamed them all. A third of the family property has been squandered, and the portion remaining, his own share, must now sustain them all. The younger brother will live on what belongs to the older, and the whole village is dining on part of it now! He is being robbed, and the little crook is the toast of the town. His response is an effort at sabotage. A refusal to join such a feast is not just an act of private sulking; it functions publicly to shame his father and his wastrel son. As the father's honoring of the prodigal aims a strong message of acceptance to the community, the elder son's boycott aims a strong message of disdain for all to heed.[11] Both sons have now publicly shamed their father and each other.

And the father, once more, is open-armed to it all. He acts toward his older son exactly as he did toward the younger. He goes to him, leaving his own feast, which again would shame him in the eyes of others. Instead of upbraiding his son, as a father in that culture would do, he pleads with him to come in. Pleading with this son is as incongruous as running to the other was—maternal behavior once more.[12] The son's response is furious. Unlike his brother (vv. 12, 21), he does not call this man "father," but says: "Listen!" (*idou*, "Look!") His ensuing complaint is less about his brother's behavior than his father's unfairness.

His perspective is phrased in the language of master and slave: "All these years I have *slaved [douleuō]* for you, and I have never disobeyed your *command*." As the younger son came applying for servitude, the older son claims to have lived in it always. He accuses his father of stinginess: "You have never given me even a young goat so that I might celebrate with my friends." This is the parable's third reference to giving.[13] "Give me," said the younger son to a compliant father (v. 12); and in a distant land, "no one gave him anything" (v. 16). Now the father is likened to those foreigners, "You have never given me...." The celebration he craves, we notice, is not with family but with "my friends." He can say "my friends," but he won't say "my brother." "This son of yours" is language distancing him from his father and that other son. And he smears him—he has "eaten up your living with prostitutes." No such thing had been said by the story. The older son is guessing, conjuring the worst, piling on shame to undo the honor bestowed by the father. "And you killed the fatted calf for him!"

Is this last line true? No doubt, the older son believes it. But, in fact, it is not the prodigal's feast; it is the father's feast. He has given it for all, for his household and for the community too. It is given also for the older son to enjoy, a feast for the wholeness of them all.

As with the younger son, the father speaks the final word. As before, the words contain not the slightest rebuke but a generous, sweeping assurance of sonship. "Son [*teknon*, child, a designation of affection], you are always with me, and all that is mine is yours." The father calls this son his companion and co-owner of everything.[14] The construct of slaving is swept away. This son owns it all. If the father never "gave" him a goat, it was because the herds, the land, the house, and all else are fully given to him. It is, once more, a shocking response. We had expected that the "underdog" prodigal would be elevated at the expense of the more privileged, resentful older brother. The first listeners, steeped in biblical stories of upstart younger sons being favored over older sons, would have expected Jesus' story to make the same move,[15] especially in view of his famous love for outsiders. But this parable subverts even that expectation. This father excludes no one, not even the righteous resentful.

As for the party in progress, he declares, "It was necessary to celebrate and rejoice." Translations often supply the word "we" here, which is not in the Greek. The emphasis is on the insistent necessity of joy. The feast is for a family, indeed, for a community made whole. "This brother of yours," he says, echoing the phrase "this son of yours," tossing kinship back to his angry son. The celebration is for nothing less than a miracle; it is, in the father's eyes, a feast of resurrection: "He was dead and is alive again. He was lost and is found." And with that, the curtain abruptly rings down on a story still unfinished. We are left outside a house filled with music, standing in the shoes of someone estranged, considering his choices and ours about a glad feast of kinship that awaits our entrance.

HOMILETICAL REFLECTIONS

Some pastors may dread the prospect of preaching this parable. It is too familiar, we think. What could possibly be said that is fresh? The temptation arises to look for a new twist, something "creative" and novel. Such inclinations betray a failure of trust in the story. The truth is that a clear telling of it, attending to the real circumstances, perspectives, and feelings described, never fails to win a fresh hearing.

Care must be taken to avoid a notorious misuse of this text, the vilification of the older son. The father doesn't beat him up—why should the preacher? The father is as kind to him as to the prodigal—in some ways, more so—and so should we be. The issue is larger than fidelity to the text. The history of preaching this parable is full of disastrous identification of the older brother with the Jewish people who rejected Jesus, an equation with no merit.[16] The identification has gone so deep that vilifying him, even without calling him a Pharisee, perpetuates dishonest and dangerous anti-Judaism. More immediately, the preacher's own audience is likely full of people who identify strongly with the older brother—dutiful people whose experience with indulged, ruinous relatives may have left them baffled, if not bitter. Failure to stand as sympathetically as possible with the older son and to show the father's unqualified love for him deprives them of any real invitation to the party.

Neither son, however, should be excused his meanness. The truth is that both sons are stinkers. Modern sensibilities may incline a preacher to indulge in psychological justifications for the choices of one or both. Such speculations do not serve the force of the parable, which concerns a parent's scandalous love of two failed children. Though the paths they take differ, they are more alike than unalike. They are both masters at sticking it to their father and to each other. The parable actually invites, in the self-indulgence of one and the rage of the other, identification with both; the sermon may offer both as a two-paneled mirror on our complicated selves.[17] Though we need not revile either, if we cannot see what is finally vicious in them (and us), we will never see sharply enough the contrasting startling kindness of the parable's central figure.

Unlike either son, the father does not orbit himself. While they obsess on their share of things, he abandons his honor, is a fool for their sakes. And he alone is spontaneous. Both sons exercise calculation about coming home—the younger must devise and rehearse a speech, the older angrily balks—but the father is all instant, uncalculated, outreaching welcome. He is a burning *purity*, a stunning simplicity of acceptance. The actions of the sons exert continuous pressure on him—and certainly on us—to choose between them, to elevate one above the other. Steadfastly, he offers equal profusions of affectionate mercy to both.

Like him, any sermon on this parable must subvert an "either/or" construct of the family of God. Each of us, with our differing temperaments, biases, and favored sins, will want to stand with one son more than the other, to tell one's tale at the expense of the other and assign one sort of sinner to greater jeopardy. This father won't allow it. In the end it is not the story of either son or of any of us. It is his story, all of it. So we must preach it all and preach it finally from where he stands, at the center of wild music, dancing, and the final feast, already in progress, that makes a place at the table for all.

CHAPTER TEN

On Preaching Parables

What does it mean to preach the parables of Jesus? What commitments and strategies pertain to preaching them well? In this book such questions have never been far from view. In our discussions of eight particular parables, some answers and patterns have begun to emerge. Now we gather up what we have learned and give further thought to the good work of getting the parables heard.

FIRST PRINCIPLES FOR PREACHERS OF PARABLES

We begin with a candid admission: *parables resist preaching; they elude our efforts to make sermons of them.* True, the parables seem accessible, alluring, and rich in the promise of meaning. They *dare* us to preach them; we want to take the dare. We have heard them preached to strong effect. Clearly, parables can and must be preached. Then why say that they resist preaching? The central problem is that a parable is, in a way at least, complete in itself. A parable is a plot (or implied plot), tightly constructed and carefully designed to do something (perhaps many things) in its hearers. Its effect is inseparable from its form. A parable is its own strategy; it is an experience and an impact. Can a joke be explained and still function as joke? If a speaker breaks in on a work of music to tell us what it means, is something lost? Something may well be gained by comment on a piece of music or a poem or a joke, but however useful the elaboration, the thing itself remains apart, does what it does on its own terms, and does much more than whatever may be said of it. Little wonder that as astute a scholar and preacher as Leander Keck could say, "Whenever I teach or preach the parables of Jesus, I feel more uneasy than with other kinds of texts."[1]

One way to state the problem is in terms of a parable's movement, which may be considerable. The plot moves, often abruptly and in very strange directions. The minds of the listeners, carried by the plot, often startled by the sharpness or seeming absurdities of its turns, undergo their own unsettling shifts. And because the parable in its total effect can spin out such a dizzying array of questions, objections, connections, implications, and applications, the "meaning" of it may be a starburst of possibilities. The thing will not stay still.

To what shall we compare a parable? It is like a river rushing forward, sharply turning, steeply falling, spinning eddies, washing many banks, flashing many lights, broadening and dividing to a delta toward the sea. How do you preach a river? The best you can do is ride it, having others ride it with you, feeling its force together, pointing to some of the sights, respecting its expansive, moving wildness, knowing it will defeat all efforts to sum it up. Preaching parables requires such an awed respect. We embark with a cheerful humility. It is a fine thing to be defeated by a parable.

Such respect implies an essential commitment: *a parable must not be lost in the preaching of it.* Whatever must be said about the parable or around it or from it, it should be experienced in the sermon *as parable.* The story need not be told all at once; its telling may span the whole sermon. But however it is done, the parable must get *traveled through*, its force and movement felt. The story is not disposable or reducible to a point or a set of points. We do not tell it and discard it to say a few words about it. All elements of the sermon will seek to serve the parable's unfolding of itself.

Paul Ricoeur described the narrative parable as "an itinerary of meaning, a signifying dynamism."[2] A sermon on such a parable honors the "itinerary of meaning" by taking the trip. The "dynamism" is kept dynamic by letting the story have its movement and play, not pinning it down to one static point or several. Fred Craddock has said that reducing a parable to a thesis in a sermon is "a violation comparable to giving children the themes or points to bedtime stories as a substitute for the stories themselves."[3] The preaching of any parable, then, will honor it by fully retaining it. We will be at pains not to bury the story beneath our talk of it. One way or another, the sermon will be a re-presentation of the parable itself.

Such a commitment has implications for how listeners are engaged. *In preaching parables we grant ample room for listeners to react, think, and wonder, to draw connections and conclusions of their own.* A parable places great responsibility on its hearers. It does not tell us what it means but pushes us to consider what it means. For preachers to make heavy-handed declarations of a parable's meaning or application, preempting the listeners' interpretive part, is false to a parable's intent. Recall Dodd's definition, which describes a parable's function as "arresting the hearer by its vividness or strangeness, and leaving the mind in sufficient doubt about its precise application to tease it into active thought."[4] The sermon follows the parable's lead, lets the teasing of the mind have its play, steadfastly allows and promotes "active thought."

To a considerable degree, of course, facilitating active engagement and reflection on the part of listeners is key to all good preaching. Many kinds of biblical texts invite it, postmodern sensibilities want it, the integrity of the church needs it, and the very nature of the gospel requires it. Parables, however, provide uniquely pointed occasions for letting listeners do their own imaginative, reflective work. With respect to engaging the listener's active imagination, we might say that preaching parables is like preaching any poetic or metaphorical or visionary or narrative text—only more so.

Like other biblical texts, a parable not only says something; it *does* something. The sermon should aim to do what the parable does. Each parable has its own distinctive function—to amaze at divine extravagance, to convict of our need for grace, to prompt obedience to divine command, to warn against naive impatience—but all of them function as well to invite or provoke us into active personal and communal engagement, reaction, reflection, and response. This is not merely the parables' method; it is at the center of their gift. A parable sermon will follow this function. We will not say all that we think we know, but give listeners the gift of their freedom and responsibility to imagine, to connect, to conclude, to choose.

How is this done? *What a parable leaves open, we do not close.* The parables of Jesus are spare in detail. Their language is lean, the narratives taut, withholding much and leaving many open questions. These silences are essential to a parable's strategy. To preach a parable rightly is largely a matter of respecting its strategic silences.

Recall, for example, our discussion of the parable of the dishonest manager. The man is accused to his master by others. Is he guilty or not? The story doesn't say. Why is he silent when accused? The story doesn't say. What is he really up to in reducing the clients' debts? The story isn't clear. As we saw, these ambiguities of detail may have strategic uses. Instead of closing them off by declaring him guilty (or not), asserting his reason for silence, and "clarifying" his subsequent actions, a preacher will better serve the parable and its hearers by leaving these matters open, raising possibilities, asking questions, opening spaces for listeners to enter, consider, and perhaps locate themselves. Or again, is the prodigal son "really" repentant or not? You will find interpreters insisting that he is not and others insisting that he is. The parable itself leaves the matter open, and for good reason. We are headed for a party that is subject to doubt and critique. So the narrative *overhears* the boy's speech and *shows* him going home, but permits us to wonder about his reasons. Respect for the story and for its hearers means not asserting what his motives are but pointing perhaps to what may or may not be so, letting listeners puzzle through the ambiguities of sinners, like themselves, headed homeward. Such silences are not passed over but entered and sensitively probed.

Other silences in the parables should largely be left alone. "An enemy has done this," says a farmer over his weed-infested field, and the preacher is unwise who launches into a dissertation on the devil. When a parable alludes in metaphor to a theological mystery, we let the metaphor do its own suggestive work, not saying more than it allows.[5] Another kind of silence to be kept pertains to any supposed psychological makeup of the characters. Many preachers like to suppose what a parabolic character feels and why. Rarely, a parable will clearly disclose a character's feelings—the older brother is said to be angry; those who worked twelve hours in the vineyard are clearly angry. But to ascribe feelings and especially to psychologize a character's motives is alien to the world of a parable and invariably weakens its force.[6] The parables are streamlined plots, not psychodramas; they deal in choices, not therapeutic issues. Here again, we keep a silence that the parable keeps.

A parable's omissions are deliberate. Its ambiguities and mysteries are openings, silent rooms for listeners to enter for confrontation, consideration, and response, for offering speech of their own. They are empty spaces for the Spirit. John Dominic Crossan has said, "Parables give God room."[7] To preach parables in a way that refuses to close what they leave open is to honor the room they give for God.

Jesus gave God room in the parables for massive rearrangements, the demolition of old worlds and the raising up of new ones. *Parables must be preached with a keen eye for radical reversals of assumptions, values, and social systems.* Often reduced to harmless moralisms and devotional tidbits, the parables are, on the whole, subversive speech. They spring devastating surprises. They stand us on ground we thought we knew, then shake it hard, upending us. We look up to an altered world, upside down to the one we knew. Starved bums are the honorees here, God is patently unfair here, devout people leave church lost here, rooting out bad seed is forbidden here, and we who had asked how to be good neighbors are in need here, it turns out, of the neighborliness of our enemies. When preparing to preach a parable, we look for the subversion in it. When we find it, we grant it full and radical force on ourselves and in our preaching.

We do not always find it. Jesus employed parables for more than one purpose; a few are more illustrative than subversive.[8] Not all of them shock.[9] But a subversive surprise is usually there, even when, to our eyes, all seems quite simple. We may assume that the tiny mustard seed growing to a big shrub simply means that miniscule beginnings can grow to sizeable results, or that a woman hiding leaven in the dough points simply to the transforming power of a small, living influence; but as we have seen, both of these parables possess a dynamism of meaning that is much more complex and startling.[10]

Being alert for the ground-shaking surprise (and doing our homework), we often find it, waving and shouting, obvious after all. Our strategy in preaching such parables is the resetting of the traps that Jesus laid and springing the surprise. Our aim, of course, is not the dramatic effect. Our aim is the radical reimaging of God's world as proclaimed by Jesus and the conversion of the church to live in the vision of that world and no other.

A final principle concerns the communal character of parable interpretation. *In attempting to hear a parable, we consult as wide a community of respondents as possible.*

As we have seen, parables are not simple. They are rich metaphorical systems, highly suggestive, inviting considerable reflection from the individuals and communities that hear them. Typically, they offer multiple trajectories of meaning and application. This being so, no single individual, or group of like-minded individuals, is likely to discern all that a parable seeks to say and do.

The problem can be stated in more negative terms. Every reader has his or her biases and blind spots. Inevitably, our culture, our theology, and our life experience will incline us to see—and not see—certain aspects, angles, and implications of a text. I am white, male, middle-aged, a Baptist, a citizen of the United States, a person, in other words, who was formed from a limited set of perspectives and, not unimportantly, from a position of social privilege. I read texts from a certain social location, and so do you. Imagine all that we cannot see from the places where we sit. We need conversation with people who sit elsewhere.[11]

Though this issue pertains to the hearing of any biblical text, it is intensified in the hearing of Jesus' parables. In the first place, he told them to people whose context and social locations were quite different from our own. Our understanding of the parables will be enhanced and often radically altered both by studying the social and economic circumstances of the parables' first hearers and by learning how they are heard among contemporary groups whose circumstances have much in common with theirs.[12] Beyond this is the broader reality that because parables are so open-ended, they are peculiarly subject to skewed readings. Some people, perhaps ourselves, perhaps some scholars and parable specialists, will see things in them that are not there. So we must be judicious. We do not interpret parables unassisted, nor do we consult a book or two and proceed to the sermon as if the meaning of the thing were clenched. We seek a wide conversation, letting various perspectives inform, expand, and correct each other.

Not to be neglected are perspectives to be found within our own congregations. Preparation for preaching a parable might include inviting a diverse group to study it and respond with their own questions, impressions, and insights. A "talk-back" following the sermon may also be fruitful and is entirely consistent with the character and function of parables. A recent school of thought suggests that Jesus told parables in part to prompt discussion among his hearers.[13] Whether or not we convene such actual conversations, we are wise when preparing to preach parables to consider a variety of perspectives, to hear many voices making answer to the teller of parables.

AN ONGOING INTERPRETIVE QUESTION

We have just spoken of multiple perspectives on the parables and of our need to give them a generous and judicious hearing. The earliest perspectives available to us are those of the Gospel writers themselves. Jesus told his parables in Aramaic, perhaps to differing audiences in differing versions. The Evangelists wrote Greek versions of them, fixing them in definite words and contexts. Drawing on traditions and sources available to them, they also employed their own distinctive vocabulary, motifs, and theological accents. Their placement of parables in particular contexts is itself an interpretive act. And sometimes outright interpretations are supplied. In other words, when we meet the parables of Jesus in the pages of Scripture, we do not find them in some pristine state; they are already, to some extent and in varying degrees, interpreted. What does this mean for the preaching of them? We have already addressed this question regarding particular parables, but a fuller discussion of the issue may be useful.

A first principle is this: Scripture is essentially what we preach; the norm for preaching parables is to attend to the words and contexts supplied in the Gospels. We preach from the canon; the church has charged us with interpreting its texts. And the texts are *given*; they are what we have. Efforts at getting "behind" the text to what Jesus really said or meant are fraught with supposition and vulnerable to projection and best guesses. Much of the current literature on the parables is aimed at recovering a lost original intention of Jesus. This is work worth doing, but the results seem often strained. The norm for preaching is to work from the texts as we have them.

This does not mean, however, that we are rigidly bound to every aspect of an Evangelist's presentation of a parable. A parable's expansive potential for meaning may exceed what a Gospel can point to. For example, Luke says that Jesus told the parable of the widow and the judge (18:2-5) to address the disciples' "need to pray always and not to lose heart" (18:1). Yes. The widow is persistent and fearless in pleading her case; and the sermon, following Luke's lead, will proclaim a God who honors prayers of passionate petition and protest. But the *terms* of the parable concern justice, the institutions that fail to deliver it, and the people who are most vulnerable to injustice. Are these elements of the story just the disposable trappings of a tale that encourages prayer? Can God be discerned in the parable, not just as the antitype of a corrupt judge, but as One who cries out in this widow and billions like her? Is she just a cipher for us all, or is she excluded in a way we are not, waiting with others like her to be joined by us in a broader advocacy? I don't know. But such questions spin out from the parable, which is, as Luke says, about prayer—and perhaps much more. In such a case, we honor a Gospel's summary of a parable's meaning and are free to go beyond it.

What of the larger issue of a parable's context within a Gospel? Current literature on the parables often counsels against taking the Gospel context into much account. My counsel is to take these contexts quite seriously. The parables, as we have them, are integrated parts of a Gospel's larger proclamation, and their contexts hold them in a web of connections that are often crucial. Richard Lischer has rightly critiqued the "aesthetic" approach that isolates parables (and other narratives) from their contexts in Scripture, theology, church, and history. Such isolation "atomizes the community's experience of the gospel—of which texts are organic parts. There is a certain genius in the connectedness of things in the Gospels."[14]

In this book we have often seen that the surrounding Gospel material sheds invaluable, legitimate light on a parable. The Samaritan parable works as it does largely because of the dialogue that frames it. Elements of Mark 4:1-10 provide illuminating continuities and contrasts for interpreting the parable of the seed thrown on the ground (Mark 4:26-29). The parables of Matthew 13, despite their distinct differences, inform one another. Luke's continuing emphasis on poverty and wealth gives added resonance to each of his several parables featuring the rich or the poor. Other examples of valid and provocative contextual light on the parables abound.

But we have also encountered real problems relative to Gospel context. The parable of the dishonest manager (Luke 16:1-8*a*) is best preached apart from the sayings that follow in verses 9-13, though Luke probably sees them as shedding light on the parable. Matthew's context for the parable of the talents (25:14-30) makes it a parable of the parousia of Christ, a setting that sharply limits the sense of the parable. And the allegorical interpretation that follows the parable of the weeds (Matt 13:24-30, 36-43) actually leads us away from the character and essence of the parable itself.

My conclusion about the Gospel contexts of parables is that we take them seriously, letting them shed all possible good light on the parables we preach. But taking them seriously does not bind us to them always or wholly. Critical discernment and common sense may require certain separations. In the service of Scripture and of the gospel of Jesus Christ, we are to be that responsible.

The same principle holds for the particular words, plot details, and theological accents supplied by the Evangelists. We take all of them into serious account, making free and generous use of the added gifts they give to a parable's sense; but discernment may be required as to how much weight the sermon gives them. Such a commitment has special bearing on parables that appear in different Gospels with varying details. Luke's version of the parable of the mustard seed (13:18-19; cf. Mark 4:30-32; Matt 13:31-32) is unique in saying that it is planted "in the garden." As noted above, this detail has truly scandalous importance; a sermon on this text will make full use of this detail. On the other hand, both Luke and Matthew refer to the mustard plant as a tree, which it simply is not. This detail, if not overtly corrected in the sermon, is laid aside. In the parable of the talents (Matt 25:14-30; cf. Luke 19:12-27), as we have seen,[15] some of the distinctively Matthean elements are rightly given full voice, while others may be more muted in the sermon. Sometimes a distinctive word or detail seems at first glance to be insignificant, but rich implications may be rightly inferred. For instance, in the parable of the tenants (Mark 12:1-8; Matt

21:33-41; Luke 20:9-16), the versions of Matthew and Mark report that the vineyard owner, after the tenants murdered his messengers, says to himself, "They will respect my son." In Luke's version, he says, "*Perhaps* they will respect him." In that single word *perhaps* the mind of the vineyard owner opens to a new pathos. He acts here not on assumption but on a poignant hope.[16] He is pondering the dreadful risk and choosing, even so, to take it. He risks his son on the anguished hope of *perhaps*.

The richest possibilities for interpretation lie in close readings of the parables as we have them in the Gospels, attending carefully to their contexts, semantics, and narrative details. We have acknowledged limits to this approach. In the case of some parables, aspects of the Gospel's presentation are best muted or transcended. And the text itself must be augmented with knowledge of historical, political, religious, and socioeconomic realities that underlie it. But given these disciplines and commitments, we return again and again to the norm and the treasure of the text as given in the Gospels.

STRATEGIES IN PREACHING PARABLES

Our first strategic concern is the structure or *form* of the parable sermon. We have already addressed this issue in general and with respect to particular parables. We certainly need not impose one all-purpose form for every parable sermon. The peculiarities of each parable, as well as our audience, the context-in-time of the sermon, and our own intuitions, will suggest differences in approach. We may consider it standard, however, that an effective course will generally be for the form of the sermon to follow the form of the story itself, though not in a wooden way.

David Buttrick gives good advice here. He counsels against a verse-by-verse approach, which tends to atomize a parable. Going line by line and word by word yields something like a commentary, not a living sermon. The result is tedious, a string of separate exegetical and theological points. The dramatic movement of the parable is dissipated, and the impact of the whole is lost. He suggests instead that the sermon move episodically, from one scene in the story to another. He advises us to "preach as if we and our congregations are hearing and reacting to the parable together. The sermon can then move along, episode by episode, like a good story, yet permit us to respond, thinking through each episode as it is heard."[17] The sermon is structured according to scenes from the parable, with comment, analogies, reactions, and summations along the way. Briefer parables, the one-liners, have fewer scenes or implied scenes. Sermons on them can be structured on what images and developments occur, with added movements of thought exploring implications and applications of the parable.

In longer narrative parables, we need not give every scene a separate development in the sermon. Like all good folktales, fairy tales, and jokes, the narrative parables make generous use of repetition. Recall our comments about the priest and the Levite bypassing the wounded traveler. They are mostly setups for the shock of the ministering enemy. We need not linger to berate them, and we certainly do not treat them as two episodes. We take sad note of them and of what they lead us to expect in a third traveler, and we move on to the parable's main disconcerting business.

This returns us to an issue mentioned early in the book that pertains to the interpretation of a parable and to the shaping of a sermon on it. We look for the parable's center of gravity, the part of its narrative where the greater stress lies. As a rule the most useful clue lies in noticing where the pace slows down and the most words are expended. So we discovered that the center of gravity in the parable of Mark 4:26-29 lies in the mysterious "automatic" growing of the seed, described in expansive detail. The parable of the rich man and Lazarus has its gravitational center in the dialogue with father Abraham, by far the longest part of the narrative. Such discernments guide us in determining where to place the weight in the sermon design, where to allot more time, perhaps, and apply the sharper accent.

Getting the parable a fresh hearing may sometimes invite a reordering of the episodes. We are not bound to telling the story in strict sequence. We may ask what, for our listeners, is the most effective entry point for getting the parable heard. We may choose to begin with the most problematic moment in the parable or with the moment with which our audience will most strongly identify, positively or negatively, then work back through the story.[18] Or if the parable's accent does not fall at its end, we may delay that portion to the end or reprise it there. The sermon sequence need not replicate the parable's sequence if, in our context, a different order better serves the parable's purpose.

At several points in this book we have addressed the need to establish appropriate *identification* with certain characters.[19] This is a vital concern, especially among people familiar with the stories. The usual problem is that a character who comes out poorly in a parable is seen by listeners from the start as *wrong*. This is not just because they know the outcome. Previous sermons or Sunday school lessons have robbed them of seeing these characters whole, flattening them to cartoon villains and dolts. The result is a safe, judgmental distance, a lost capacity to see these figures as our kin. We identify instead with characters that the parables vindicate— that sweetly penitent tax collector, for instance. Original hearers of Jesus' parables had no such confusion. When he showed them a Pharisee and a tax collector, they saw a saint and a rat. His parables worked precisely because his audience rightly understood the types he presented and so were rightly surprised by the reversals he sprang.

Our task is to get the types rightly perceived, to foster affinities with characters we had thought to disdain, to show the parables' "heroes" for the bums they may be. Consulting sound biblical scholarship grants a truer sense of the cultural types Jesus employed in his parables. But such data should not be heavily dumped into the sermon. Lengthy history lessons about Pharisees derail narrative movement and may widen the distance we want to narrow. Brief historical comment will do. Real identification can then be achieved by contemporary analogy. We ask ourselves who in our world may be admirably like the Pharisees—volunteers in community service; generous donors; people who teach Sunday school, serve as deacons, pray, give thanks for their blessings; people whose commitments hold a community together. Only by appreciating his strengths can we notice what's really off about him, and perhaps us. Only by sniffing the stink on the tax-taking traitor can the scandal of the parable have its say.

The issue of identification is not always about "bad" and "good" characters. Where we locate ourselves in the parable—call it point of view—can determine its very meaning. The point of the Samaritan parable is totally changed if instead of trying to identify with the priest, Levite, or Samaritan, we locate ourselves with the man in the ditch. The accent then shifts, as the text seems to do, from whom do we help to whom do we need. Or consider the parable of the sower. It is often preached so as to ask: what kind of *soil* are we—hardened path, rocky, thorny, or good and receptive? It is a very different parable if it is asking: what kind of *farmers* are we? Locating ourselves with that rather careless flinger of seeds, seeing so much waste, we are led to amazed delight at the bounty of the harvest even so, and to join in God's indiscriminate sowing, undeterred by manifest failures, smiling at the inexorable harvest coming still.

Certain qualities of *style* in the parables may inform our style in preaching them. One of these is spareness—lean language prompting quick movements of thought and plot. Why not follow suit? Meandering descriptions, surplus adjectives and adverbs, wordy asides—these are bad choices in any event but especially weaken the preaching of parables. Remember, parables *evoke*. Their tautness and abruptness serve the purpose. Our words, disciplined, may do the same.

Another quality of parabolic style is earthy concreteness. Parables are not, as used to be said, simple stories from everyday life; but the scenery, characters, customs, institutions, and social systems they adduce were the common stuff of the actual world of the hearers. For them, a denarius, a Pharisee, and the road from Jerusalem to Jericho were as ordinary as a dollar, a deacon, and I-75 are for us. The parables worked by the collision of this concretely recognized familiar world with the strange, alternative in-breaking world of God. For parables to work in our preaching, the same collision should occur.

We cannot accomplished this by merely translating the concrete cultural elements from the parable to cultural elements of our own. Real cultural equivalents may not exist. In our little sample list above, a dollar, a deacon, and I-75 are inadequate analogies to a denarius, a Pharisee, and the road from Jerusalem to Jericho. Aspects of the originals that are essential to their stories are absent from any modern substitute. So what do we do? We *mix* worlds. On the one hand, we take real account of the first-century elements of the parable. We offer words that shine a light on the real Jericho road, the unit of currency called a talent, the power arrangements of a steward's world. We do this as nimbly as we can. We shun the long excursus in favor of the quick sketch. While giving our listeners a sense of original conditions, we do not want to resettle them in Bible-land. The story unfolds in their world too. So along with references to original terms, we stir in generous portions of starkly contemporary terms.

At one level, we do this through concrete analogy. The Pharisee morphs to a soup kitchen volunteer, a saintly Sunday school teacher, a generous donor. The Samaritan looks suspiciously like a terrorist or perhaps, for some congregations, a gay man with AIDS. A master entrusting talents to slaves is a CEO writing checks to employees for two-and-a-half million dollars, a million, and half a million.

But analogy may not be enough. To mix worlds thoroughly, we can playfully slip deliberate anachronisms into the story. To the farmer with a field full of darnel come slaves holding weed-whackers. The prodigal squeals off in a red Lamborghini. He passes a road sign that says, "FAR COUNTRY: CLOSER THAN YOU THINK."[20] I once heard a sermon that showed the rich man dining on onion soup, salad with blue cheese dressing, beef Wellington with a vintage wine, baked potato, and fresh asparagus, followed by cherries jubilee and a hot cup of coffee.[21] My stomach growled. This kind of play in a sermon is fun; it's the fun of *recognition*. Such vividness of concrete, current detail—props and people we know popping up in the parables—draws us in, startles us to a new participation. There is something unsettling about it too. The safely removed biblical world flickers strangely to our own. The parable's fierce collision is headed toward *us*. The wreckage will be local. Sorting through the pieces and deciding where they go happens in the room, in the parking lot, in all the real places where we live.

THE LIMITS AND PROMISE OF PARABLE

Parables are metaphors of God. Speaking them, Jesus was "throwing alongside" (*para-bolē*) the Infinite these earthy images and strange plots. "To what shall I liken it?" he kept saying, and the people leaned forward. "It is like...."

Such an enterprise has its limits: "To whom will you liken me and make me equal, and compare me, as though we were alike?" (Isa 46:5). No image encapsulates God; no metaphor is adequate to divine mystery. This is why Jesus, like the prophets, sages, and psalmists before him, could not limit his figurative speech for God to one or two metaphors but sang out a superabundance of them.[22] He did not "throw alongside" God an image and say, "There it is!" He flung great sprays of them, like stars, and left us looking up in wonder.

We read and preach parables under that sense of immensity, knowing that no single one of them says enough about God or even about ourselves. So we do not press them too far, do not make their images "graven." Following the lead of the Scriptures and of Jesus, we move from image to image and text to text, granting the witness of each *and* of the whole vast, many-colored constellation of them all. Together the parables orbit the divine mystery, flashing images of female and male, royalty and servanthood, enemy and friend, power and impoverishment, scandal and triumph, devastation and joy, harsh verdicts and dazzling generosities. We hear and preach what each of them sings; we hear and preach the whole chorus they make—harmonies, dissonance, and all.

Even this falls short. Had it been sufficient, Jesus could have kept spinning out parables into his old age. Ultimately, what he "threw alongside" the divine mystery was his life. All along, while telling parables, he lived one. His friendships, healings, prophetic actions, and choice of dinner companions were embodied parables. His ultimate parable was his death. It seems more than slightly significant that the only two universally accepted historical facts about Jesus are that he was a parable maker and that he was crucified.[23] These two facts are of a piece. His parables were dangerous. And the laying down of daring parabolic action and speech anticipates—and is—the laying down of life.

The parables keep pointing beyond themselves to such a way of living. And they give us good equipment for it. Their insistent way of exposing and wrecking old systems gives us critical distance for the courage we need to renounce the claims of such systems on us and on others. Their imaginative vision lights the fires of the burning communal imagination that fuels and sustains a living faith. Their miraculous, impossible stretching of speech lays down a pattern for the stretching of our language and the stretching of our common life toward more daring expression of the inexpressible. To preach the parables is to claim such gifts, to practice them, to live them, to impart them. "Follow me," said Jesus, then gave us parables, spoken and lived. And so we follow.

Notes

1. Into the World of the Parables

1. Thomas G. Long, *Preaching and the Literary Forms of the Bible* (Philadelphia: Fortress Press, 1989), 87.

2. Bernard Brandon Scott, *Hear Then the Parable* (Minneapolis: Fortress Press, 1989), 14.

3. See, for example, Brad H. Young, *Jesus and His Jewish Parables* (Mahwah, N.J.: Paulist Press, 1989), and his *The Parables: Jewish Tradition and Christian Interpretation* (Peabody, Mass.: Hendrickson, 1998). Young expresses indebtedness to David Flusser.

4. Joachim Jeremias, *The Parables of Jesus* (trans. S. H. Hooke; 2nd rev. ed.; New York: Charles Scribner's Sons, 1972), 12.

5. George Arthur Buttrick, *The Parables of Jesus* (New York: Harper & Brothers, 1928), xiv.

6. David Stern, *Parables in Midrash: Narrative and Exegesis in Rabbinic Literature* (Cambridge, Mass.: Harvard University Press, 1991), 93.

7. A recent book by Bernard Brandon Scott is aptly titled *Re-Imagine the World: An Introduction to the Parables of Jesus* (Santa Rosa, Calif.: Polebridge Press, 2001).

8. C. H. Dodd, *The Parables of the Kingdom* (rev. ed.; New York: Charles Scribner's Sons, 1961).

9. Dan Otto Via Jr., *The Parables: Their Literary and Existential Dimension* (Philadelphia: Fortress Press, 1967). This line of interpretation had been partially explored by Geraint V. Jones, *The Art and Truth of the Parables* (London: S.P.C.K., 1964).

10. Among the seminal early works on these lines were Amos N. Wilder, *The Language of the Gospel: Early Christian Rhetoric* (New York: Harper & Row, 1964), 79-96; Robert W. Funk, *Language, Hermeneutic, and Word of God* (New York: Harper & Row, 1966), 133-62; John Dominic Crossan, *In Parables: The Challenge of the Historical Jesus* (New York: Harper & Row, 1973); and Paul Ricoeur, "Biblical Hermeneutics," *Semeia* 4 (1975): 29-148.

11. See, for example, Robert W. Funk, Bernard Brandon Scott, and James R. Butts, *The Parables of Jesus: Red Letter Edition, A Report of the Jesus Seminar* (Sonoma,

Calif.: Polebridge Press, 1982); Scott, *Hear Then the Parable;* and the various works of John Dominic Crossan.

12. See William R. Herzog II, *Parables as Subversive Speech: Jesus as Pedagogue of the Oppressed* (Louisville: Westminster/John Knox Press, 1994), and V. George Shillington, ed., *Jesus and His Parables: Interpreting the Parables of Jesus Today* (Edinburgh: T&T Clark, 1997).

13. Scott, *Hear Then the Parable*, 42.

14. David Buttrick, *Speaking Parables: A Homiletic Guide* (Louisville: Westminster John Knox Press, 2000), 19.

15. Wilder, *Language of the Gospel*, 86, 74.

16. Scott, *Hear Then the Parable*, 381-83.

17. Jeremias stressed that the parables create a crisis of decision: "all the parables of Jesus compel his hearers to come to a decision about his person and his message" (*Parables of Jesus*, 231).

18. Dodd, *Parables of the Kingdom*, 5.

19. Ron Hansen, *A Stay Against Confusion: Essays on Faith and Fiction* (New York: HarperCollins, 2001), 11.

20. Robert Francis, *The Orb Weaver* (Wesleyan University Press, 1960); reprinted in *The Rag and Bone Shop of the Heart* (ed. Robert Bly, James Hillman, and Michael Meade; New York: HarperCollins, 1992), 187.

21. The chapters of this book that deal with individual parables bear titles that are simply a portion of the parable's opening line. In this, I am following the lead of Bernard Brandon Scott.

22. G. K. Chesterton, *Orthodoxy* (Garden City, N.Y.: Doubleday, Image Books Edition, 1955), 146.

23. Ricoeur, "Biblical Hemeneutics," 114, 118.

24. Flannery O'Connor, *Mystery and Manners: Occasional Prose* (ed. Sally and Robert Fitzgerald; New York: Farrar, Straus & Giroux, 1961), 34.

25. Franz Kafka, *Parables and Paradoxes* (New York: Schocken Books, 1961), 11; cited by Scott, *Hear Then the Parable*, 76.

2. Someone Scatters Seed

1. Jeremias called this parable "the Patient Husbandman" in *The Parables of Jesus* (trans. S. H. Hooke; 2nd rev. ed.; New York: Charles Scribner's Sons, 1972), 151. John Dominic Crossan locates the parable's accent on the harvest, classifies it as a parable of action, and calls it "the parable of the Reaper." *In Parables: The Challenge of the Historical Jesus* (New York: Harper & Row, 1973), 84-85.

2. Barbara E. Reid, *Parables for Preachers* (Collegeville, Minn.: Liturgical Press, 1999), 64-66.

3. For a good summary of interpretations, see Peter Rhea Jones, *Studying the Parables of Jesus* (Macon, Ga.: Smyth & Helwys, 1999), 100-104.

4. A useful study devoted to interpreting the parables according to their Gospel contexts is John R. Donahue, *The Gospel in Parable* (Philadelphia: Fortress Press, 1988).

5. See Mary Ann Tolbert, *Perspectives on the Parables: An Approach to Multiple Interpretation* (Philadelphia: Fortress Press, 1979), 71, 79-81.

6. Justin, *First Apology*, 14-15; cited by Wilder, *Language of the Gospel*, 71.

7. This is a point persuasively made concerning Hebrew narrative by Robert Alter, *The Art of Biblical Narrative* (New York: Basic Books, 1981), passim. Though Alter asserts with good reason that the New Testament is written with "different literary assumptions" (ix), it seems to me that the parables of Jesus reflect some of the finest elements of Hebrew narrative.

8. David Buttrick, *Speaking Parables: A Homiletic Guide* (Louisville: Westminster John Knox Press, 2000), 72.

9. Bernard Brandon Scott says, "To the attuned hearer . . . the land is on sabbatical. The allusion is meant not literally but as a metaphorical reference to the graced character of the growth event." *Hear Then the Parable* (Minneapolis: Fortress Press, 1989), 369.

10. John Dominic Crossan, *Cliffs of Fall: Paradox and Polyvalence in the Parables of Jesus* (New York: Seabury Press, 1980), 48.

11. Scott, *Hear Then the Parable*, 369-71. This view receives a forceful homiletic treatment in Buttrick, *Speaking Parables*, 70-74.

12. C. H. Dodd, *The Parables of the Kingdom* (rev. ed.; New York: Charles Scribner's Sons, 1961), 140-44; Crossan, *In Parables*, 85; John Drury, *The Parables in the Gospels: History and Allegory* (New York: Crossroads, 1985), 59; Herman Hendrickx, *The Parables of Jesus* (San Francisco: Harper & Row, 1986), 22.

13. Eduard Schweizer, speaking of our parable, suggests, "It may be that it was omitted or changed by the later Gospel writers because it was not possible to give it a moralistic interpretation." *The Good News according to Mark* (trans. Donald H. Madvig; Atlanta: John Knox Press, 1976), 102.

14. Frederick Buechner, *Telling the Truth: The Gospel as Tragedy, Comedy, and Fairy Tale* (New York: Harper & Row, 1977), 63.

15. Peter Rhea Jones distinguishes between a parable's various implications and its "center of gravity," *Studying the Parables*, 107.

16. Andrew Harvey, *A Journey in Ladakh* (Boston: Houghton Mifflin, 1983), 93; quoted by Belden C. Lane, *The Solace of Fierce Landscapes: Exploring Desert and Mountain Spirituality* (New York: Oxford University Press, 1998), 54.

3. Two Men Went Up to the Temple

1. The parable not only ends Luke's special travel material but also bridges to what immediately follows: children dismissed by some but accepted by Jesus (18:15-17) and a rich man who departs from Jesus unchanged (18:18-30); R. Alan Culpepper, "The Gospel of Luke" (vol. 9 of *The New Interpreter's Bible*; Nashville: Abingdon, 1995), 340.

2. John R. Donahue, *The Gospel in Parable* (Philadelphia: Fortress Press, 1988), 180.

3. Fred B. Craddock, *Luke* (Interpretation; Louisville: John Knox Press, 1990), 208.

4. Ibid., 208-9.

5. Robert C. Tannehill, *Luke* (Abingdon New Testament Commentaries; Nashville: Abingdon, 1998), 266.

6. Most scholars think this saying of Jesus (also in 14:11) was added by Luke or his source to the parable, though some suggest its original place was here. Joachim Jeremias, *The Parables of Jesus* (trans. S. H. Hooke; 2nd rev. ed.; New York: Charles Scribner's Sons, 1972), 144 n. 62; I. Howard Marshall, *Commentary on Luke* (New Testament Critical Commentary; Grand Rapids: Eerdmans, 1978), 681.

7. Charles W. Hedrick notes that the parable could easily begin, "A certain Pharisee and a tax collector went up . . . ," though he believes the delay in identifying the two is "to create a little suspense." *Parables as Poetic Fictions: The Creative Voice of Jesus* (Peabody, Mass.: Hendrickson, 1994), 213.

8. Quoted by Eta Linnemann, *Parables of Jesus: Introduction and Exposition* (trans. John Sturdy; London: S.P.C.K., 1966), 58.

9. John R. Donahue, "Tax Collectors and Sinners: An Attempt at Identification," *Catholic Biblical Quarterly* 33 (1971): 39-61; also William R. Herzog II, *Parables as Subversive Speech: Jesus as Pedagogue of the Oppressed* (Louisville: Westminster/John Knox Press, 1994), 180-81; Hedrick, *Parables as Poetic Fictions*, 215-17.

10. John Dominic Crossan, *Raid on the Articulate: Comic Eschatology in Jesus and Borges* (New York: Harper & Row, 1976), 180-81.

11. For the view that he "prayed thus about himself," see Joseph A. Fitzmyer, *The Gospel according to Luke (X–XXIV)* (vol. 28A of *The Anchor Bible*; Garden City, N.Y.: Doubleday, 1985), 1186; and John Nolland, *Luke 9:21–18:34* (vol. 35b of the Word Biblical Commentary; Dallas: Word Books, 1993), 873.

12. Robert Farrar Capon, *The Parables of Grace* (Grand Rapids: Eerdmans, 1988), 179.

13. Most often cited is a prayer from the Talmud:

I thank thee, O Lord, my God, that thou has given me my lot with those who sit in the seat of learning, and not with those who sit at the street-corners; for I am early to work, and they are early to work; I am early to work on the words of the Torah, and they are early to work on things of no moment. I weary myself, and they weary themselves; I weary myself and profit thereby, while they weary themselves to no profit. I run and they run; I run towards the life of the Age to Come, and they run towards the pit of destruction. (*b. Ber. 28b*)

14. Kenneth E. Bailey, *Through Peasant Eyes* (Grand Rapids: Eerdmans, 1980), 153.

15. Ibid., 154.

16. Because the narrative is interrupted with "I tell you," some argue that v. 14 is not part of the parable, that Jesus simply described the two men at prayer and left his listeners to draw their own conclusions; Hedrick, *Parables as Poetic Fictions*, 210-11. This seems to me doubtful.

17. Nolland, *Luke*, 878.

18. David Buttrick, *Speaking Parables: A Homiletic Guide* (Louisville: Westminster John Knox, 2000), 225.

19. William Muehl preached a stinging countersermon called "The Cult of the Publican," decrying our use of texts like this one to make a career of penitence and reduce Christianity to conversionism. *All the Damned Angels* (Philadelphia: Pilgrim Press, 1972), 25-33; reprinted in *A Chorus of Witnesses* (ed. Thomas G. Long and Cornelius Plantinga Jr.; Grand Rapids: Eerdmans, 1994), 146-54.

20. Jürgen Moltmann, *The Power of the Powerless* (trans. Margaret Kohl; San Francisco: Harper & Row, 1983), 88-97; reprinted in Long and Plantinga, *Chorus of Witnesses*, 21-33.

21. I owe the link between the parable and the cleansing of the temple to Michael Farris, "A Tale of Two Taxations," in *Jesus and His Parables: Interpreting the Parables of Jesus Today* (ed. V. George Shillington; Edinburgh: T&T Clark, 1997), 31. His reading of the parable is focused on injustices in the "temple tax" system, represented by the Pharisee. The argument was earlier developed by Herzog, *Parables as Subversive Speech*, 173-93.

4. From Jerusalem to Jericho

1. Robert W. Funk, *Parables and Presence: Forms of the New Testament Tradition* (Philadelphia: Fortress Press, 1982), 65.

2. Some scholars hold that the Lucan context harms the parable; e.g., John Dominic Crossan, *In Parables: The Challenge of the Historical Jesus* (New York: Harper & Row, 1973), 58-62. In my view, the tensions between the parable and the dialogue strengthen the parable's force.

3. Ancient textual evidence for the combining of the two commandments before the time of Jesus is actually somewhat mixed. For references and the questions pertaining to them see Joseph A. Fitzmyer, *The Gospel according to Luke (X–XXIV)* (vol. 28A of *The Anchor Bible*; Garden City, N.Y.: Doubleday, 1985), 879, and John Nolland, *Luke 9:21–18:34* (vol. 35b of the Word Biblical Commentary; Dallas: Word Books, 1993), 580-82.

4. This parallel structure is delineated by Crossan, *In Parables*, 61.

5. Thomas Merton described Jesus' response as an act of mercy: "The two questions asked by the scribe were, then, useless. Therefore Christ did not answer them. Yet He did not pass them by without attention. On the contrary, He saw them as indications of the scribe's plight and of our own. Instead of answering the question, He poured oil and wine into the wounds." *Seasons of Celebration* (New York: Farrar, Straus & Giroux, 1965), 182.

6. Josephus called it a wild, desert terrain (*Jewish War*, 4.474). The Greek geographer Strabo wrote that Pompey had to destroy "strongholds of brigands" near Jericho (*Geography*, 16.2.41).

7. Robert W. Funk, "How Do You Read (Luke 10:25-37)," *Interpretation* 18 (1964): 56-61; *Language, Hermeneutic, and Word of God*, 199-222; "The Good Samaritan as Metaphor," *Semeia* 2 (1974): 74-81; *Parables and Presence*, 55-65; *Honest to Jesus: Jesus for a New Millennium* (San Francisco: Harper Collins, 1996), 170-80.

8. Funk, *Parables and Presence*, 32.

9. Charles W. Hedrick, *Parables as Poetic Fictions: The Creative Voice of Jesus* (Peabody, Mass.: Hendrickson, 1994), 105-6.

10. Nolland, *Luke*, 593.

11. On this basis, some have argued that the priest and the Levite were justified in passing by the man; e.g., J. D. Derrett, *Law in the New Testament* (London: Darton, Longman & Todd, 1970), 212-14.

12. See Bernard Brandon Scott, *Hear Then the Parable* (Minneapolis: Fortress Press, 1989), 195-96.

13. Several Talmudic references make use of the triad priest, Levite, Israelite. See ibid., 198.

14. Claude Montefiore, *The Synoptic Gospels* (London: Macmillan & Co., 1909), 2:467; cited by Scott, *Hear Then the Parable*, 198.

15. Josephus, *Jewish Antiquities*, 18.2.2.

16. Scott, *Hear Then the Parable*, 197.

17. Norman Perrin, *Jesus and the Language of the Kingdom* (Philadelphia: Fortress Press, 1976), 119, 177.

18. Arthur C. McGill, *Suffering: A Test of Theological Method* (Philadelphia: Westminster Press, 1982), 104.

19. Crossan, *In Parables*, 63.

20. *Neighbor* means this throughout the Hebrew Bible, with the possible exception of Prov 17:17; I. Howard Marshall, *Commentary on Luke* (New Testament Critical Commentary; Grand Rapids: Eerdmans, 1978), 446.

21. David Buttrick, *Speaking Parables: A Homiletic Guide* (Louisville: Westminster John Knox Press, 2000), 185.

22. Martin Luther King, Jr., *Strength to Love* (New York: Harper & Row, 1963), 20-29. For King's other treatments of the parable, see Richard Lischer, *The Preacher King: Martin Luther King, Jr. and the Word That Moved America* (New York: Oxford University Press, 1995), 101-2, 204, 206-7, 232.

23. See Walter Wink, "The Parable of the Compassionate Samaritan: A Communal Exegesis Approach," *Review and Expositor* 76, no. 2 (Spring 1979): 199-217; Ronald J. Allen, "Shaping Sermons by the Language of the Text," in *Preaching Biblically: Creating Sermons in the Shape of Scripture* (ed. Don M. Wardlaw; Philadelphia: Westminster Press, 1983), 29-59; John Claypool, *Stories Jesus Still Tells: The Parables* (2nd rev. ed.; Cambridge, Mass.: Cowley Press, 2000), 98-99.

24. For Origen, man = Adam; Jerusalem = Paradise; Jericho = world; robbers = enemies; priest = Law; Levite = prophets; Samaritan = Christ; inn = church; two denarii = Father and Son; promise to return = Parousia. For Augustine, Jerusalem = the heavenly city; Jericho = the moon, symbol of mortality; robbers = the devil and his angels; priest and Levite = the priesthood and ministry of the OT; binding the wounds = the restraint of sin; oil and wine = the comfort of hope and the encouragement to work; animal = the Incarnation; the next day = the resurrection of Christ; innkeeper = Paul; two denarii = commandments of love and promise of this life and life to come; cited by Peter Rhea Jones, *Studying the Parables of Jesus* (Macon, Ga.: Smyth & Helwys, 1999), 23-24, 297-98.

25. Robert Farrar Capon offers an alternative near-allegorical interpretation, equating Christ with the *victim* in the parable. *The Parables of Grace* (Grand Rapids: Eerdmans, 1988), 58-67. His view is followed by Mike Graves, "Luke 10:25-37: The Moral of the 'Good Samaritan' Story?" *Review and Expositor* 94, no. 2 (Spring 1997): 269-75.

26. In Chartres Cathedral there is a window in which the lower portion portrays the Samaritan parable while the upper portion depicts scenes of Creation and Fall from Gen 2-4. Other medieval cathedrals make similar juxtapositions. Allegorical equations are not being asserted, but connections are being invited within the vaulted, far-reaching context of worship. This seems to me a fair image

of what preaching the parable may finally invite. For a discussion of the Chartres window, see J. Ian H. McDonald, "Alien Grace," in *Jesus and His Parables: Interpreting the Parables of Jesus Today* (ed. V. George Shillington; Edinburgh: T&T Clark, 1997), 35-36.

5. A Man Entrusted His Money

1. Some scholars claim that vestiges of a separate parable about a "throne claimant" (Luke 19:12*b*, 14-15*a*, 27) are fused into the parable of the pounds; Joachim Jeremias, *The Parables of Jesus* (trans. S. H. Hooke; 2nd rev. ed.; New York: Charles Scribner's Sons, 1972), 59, and John Dominic Crossan, *In Parables: The Challenge of the Historical Jesus* (New York: Harper & Row, 1973), 103. But this material is sufficiently explained by Luke's own interests; Bernard Brandon Scott, *Hear Then the Parable* (Minneapolis: Fortress Press, 1989), 223; Joseph A. Fitzmyer, *The Gospel according to Luke (X–XXIV)* (vol. 28A of *The Anchor Bible*; Garden City, N.Y.: Doubleday, 1985), 1231; and Arland J. Hultgren, *The Parables of Jesus: A Commentary* (Grand Rapids: Eerdmans, 2000), 284.

2. This is not to say that Jesus himself told his parables only once. But different performances of parables by Jesus cannot fully account for the Evangelists' performances of them, marked as they are by stylistic and thematic features demonstrably their own; *contra* Richard T. France, "On Being Ready," in *The Challenge of Jesus' Parables* (ed. Richard N. Longenecker; Grand Rapids: Eerdmans, 2000), 184.

3. Wheat and tares, 13:24-30; unmerciful servant, 18:23-35; good employer, 20:1-16; two sons, 21:28-30; wedding garment, 22:11-14; bridesmaids, 25:1-13; Last Judgment, 25:31-46. Matthew repeats Mark's only parable of this type (wicked tenants, 21:33-44) and includes others from Q (two houses, 7:24-27; unclean spirit, 12:43-45; burglar, 24:43-44; slave entrusted with supervision, 24:45-51). Most telling is his use of the Great Supper parable (22:1-10; cf. Luke 14:16-24), to which he adds an epilogue parable of judgment (22:11-14).

4. John R. Donahue, *The Gospel in Parable* (Philadelphia: Fortress Press, 1988), 63.

5. Jack Dean Kingsbury, *The Parables of Jesus in Matthew 13: A Study in Redaction Criticism* (Richmond: John Knox Press, 1969), 130-37.

6. That we are intended to see a link between the two parables is indicated by the word *for (gar)* in v. 14.

7. Jennifer A. Glancy, "Slaves and Slavery in the Matthean Parables," *Journal of Biblical Literature* 119, no. 1 (Spring 2000): 67-90; and Hultgren, *Parables of Jesus*, 473-76.

8. The *mina* is worth one hundred denarii, and each of the ten slaves receives only one. Luke's parable of the "pounds" therefore lacks the shock value of entrusted talents. The shock value in Luke's parable pertains to the return on investments.

9. The 100 percent profit is not among the oversized details of Jesus' parables but is within what might be expected in that culture; J. D. Derrett, *Law in the New Testament* (London: Darton, Longman & Todd, 1970), 19-24; cited in Scott, *Hear Then the Parable*, 226 n. 41. The 1,000 percent profit in Luke's parable is a different matter.

10. In the Gamara, Rabbi Samuel says, "Money can only be guarded [by placing it] in the earth." *b. B. Mesi'a 42a*, cited by Scott, *Hear Then the Parable*, 227.

11. Josephus, *Jewish War*, 6.5.2.

12. Jeremias suggests that "enter into the joy of your master" amounts to an invitation to a feast and, in this case, to the eschatological feast of the kingdom (*Parables of Jesus*, 60 n. 42).

13. This is another distinctly Matthean expression. "Outer darkness" and "weeping and gnashing of teeth" occur in no other Gospel, and are joined three times in Matthew (8:12; 22:13; 25:30).

14. Dan Otto Via Jr., *The Parables: Their Literary and Existential Dimension* (Philadelphia: Fortress Press, 1967), 118; Bernard Brandon Scott, *Jesus, Symbol-Maker for the Kingdom* (Philadelphia: Fortress Press, 1981), 42; and Scott, *Hear Then the Parable*, 232.

15. This connection is made by Thomas G. Long, *Matthew* (Westminster Bible Companion; Louisville: Westminster John Knox Press, 1997), 283.

16. Though my assessment of the master is consistent with that of many interpreters, some hold a different view. David Buttrick finds the master in agreement with the slave that he is ruthless, making this a parable of what God is *not* like; *Speaking Parables: A Homiletic Guide* (Louisville: Westminster John Knox Press, 2000), 171-77. More radically, William R. Herzog II sees the third slave as the hero of the story because he tells the truth about the master, who exploits the peasants. Burying the talent kept some of his capital from doing its oppressive work. Herzog sees parables generally not as metaphors of God but as forms of social analysis, exploring how people could respond to economic and political oppression; *Parables as Subversive Speech: Jesus as Pedagogue of the Oppressed* (Louisville: Westminster/John Knox Press, 1994), 3, 7, 150-68.

17. The *Gospel of the Nazarenes* has not survived but is quoted by Eusebius. *New Testament Apocrypha* (ed. W. Schneemelcher and E. Hennecke; trans. R. M. Wilson; rev. ed.; Louisville: Westminster John Knox Press, 1991), 1:161-62.

18. Scott, *Hear Then the Parable*, 224 n. 33.

19. Ibid., 230-32.

20. In an essay on Matthew, John Updike relates a childhood impression in Lutheran Sunday school: "The parable of the talents bore a clear lesson for me: Live your life. Live it as if there is a blessing on it. Dare to take chances, lest you leave your talent buried in the ground. I could picture so clearly the hole that the timorous servant would dig in the dirt, and even imagine how cozily cold and damp it would feel to his hand as he placed his talent in it." *Incarnation: Contemporary Writers on the New Testament* (ed. Alfred Corn; New York: Viking Penguin, 1990), 11.

6. A Rich Man Clothed in Purple

1. Though the NRSV states "At his gate lay a poor man," the verb is actually a passive form (*ebeblēto*, literally, "thrown down"). It is an expression used of the bedridden and suggests that he was too ill or weak to take himself there. Luke Timothy Johnson paraphrases that the man was "dumped"; *The Gospel of Luke*

(Sacra Pagina, ed. Daniel J. Harrington; Collegeville, Minn.: Liturgical Press, 1991), 252.

2. Joachim Jeremias relates the Egyptian tale and the Jewish one presented here; *The Parables of Jesus* (trans. S. H. Hooke; 2nd rev. ed.; New York: Charles Scribner's Sons, 1972), 183.

3. Some scholars hold that none of the parable derives from Jesus; e.g., Rudolf Bultmann, *History of the Synoptic Tradition* (trans. John Marsh; rev. ed.; New York: Harper & Row, 1963), 196-97; and John R. Donahue, *The Gospel in Parable* (Philadelphia: Fortress Press, 1988), 170. Others maintain that only 16:19-26 comes from Jesus, the remaining verses being added by the early church to address Jewish unbelief in Jesus' resurrection; e.g., John Dominic Crossan, *In Parables: The Challenge of the Historical Jesus* (New York: Harper & Row, 1973), 67; and Bernard Brandon Scott, *Hear Then the Parable* (Minneapolis: Fortress Press, 1989), 142-46. Arguments for the whole parable deriving from Jesus are made by I. Howard Marshall, *Commentary on Luke* (New Testament Critical Commentary; Grand Rapids: Eerdmans, 1978), 634; Joseph A. Fitzmyer, *The Gospel According to Luke (X–XXIV)* (vol. 28A of *The Anchor Bible*; Garden City, N.Y.: Doubleday, 1985), 1127; William R. Herzog II, *Parables as Subversive Speech: Jesus as Pedagogue of the Oppressed* (Louisville: Westminster/John Knox Press, 1994), 116; and Peter Rhea Jones, *Studying the Parables of Jesus* (Macon, Ga.: Smyth & Helwys, 1999), 164-65.

4. R. Alan Culpepper, "The Gospel of Luke" (vol. 9 of *The New Interpreter's Bible*; Nashville: Abingdon, 1995), 316.

5. Arland J. Hultgren, *The Parables of Jesus: A Commentary* (Grand Rapids: Eerdmans, 2000), 112; Marshall, *Commentary on Luke*, 632.

6. Culpepper, "Gospel of Luke," 316. In Revelation 19:21 the verb is used for birds "gorging" on human flesh. Luke elsewhere uses the word for the longing of the hungry (6:21; 9:17; 15:16).

7. Donahue, *Gospel in Parable*, 170.

8. Scott, *Hear Then the Parable*, 152; and Hultgren, *Parables of Jesus*, 113 n. 13.

9. The point is stressed by Herzog, *Parables as Subversive Speech*, 124. In fact, Abraham had a chief servant named Eliezer (Gen 15:2). J. D. Derrett notes that certain midrashic tales describe Eliezer as still walking the earth in disguise and reporting to Abraham on how his children observed the Torah, especially in regard to caring for the poor and giving hospitality to strangers; *Law in the New Testament* (London: Darton, Longman & Todd, 1970), 78-99; cited by Donahue, *Gospel in Parable*, 169-70.

10. Herzog, *Parables as Subversive Speech*, 124. Richard L. Rohrbaugh comments, "The fact that he thinks only of his peers is one of the parable's most telling points." *The Biblical Interpreter: An Agrarian Bible in an Industrial Age* (Philadelphia: Fortress Press, 1978), 76.

11. Herzog, *Parables as Subversive Speech*, 125.

12. Many have made this point. Especially helpful discussion is given by Fred B. Craddock, *Luke* (Interpretation; Louisville: John Knox Press, 1990), 193-96.

13. Jeremias, *Parables of Jesus*, 186.

14. Commentators who make this point include, among others: E. Earle Ellis, *The Gospel of Luke* (New Century Bible; rev. ed.; London: Oliphants, 1974), 201;

Charles Talbert, *Reading Luke* (New York: Crossroads, 1982), 156-59; Culpepper, "Gospel of Luke," 315.

15. Some sample texts are: Exod 23:10-11; Deut 15:7-11; 24:10-15, 19-22; 1 Sam 2:2-7; Pss 10; 49; Isa 3:14-15; 58:6-7; Amos 2:6-7; 4:1; 5:12; 6:4-6. Psalm 49, according to some, may actually underlie the parable of the rich man and Lazarus; Jones, *Studying the Parables*, 166, following Hans-Joachim Kraus.

16. Culpepper, "Gospel of Luke," 320. For Crossan, the similarities between Luke 24 and Luke 16:27-31 constitute reason to reject 16:27-31 as coming from Jesus; *In Parables*, 67; see note 3 above.

17. For two sermons that do this very effectively, see Walter Brueggemann, "On the Wrong Side of the Ditch ... for a Long Time," in *The Threat of Life: Sermons on Pain, Power, and Weakness* (ed. Charles L. Campbell; Minneapolis: Fortress Press, 1996), 136-43; and Barbara Brown Taylor, "A Fixed Chasm," in *Bread of Angels* (Cambridge, Mass.: Cowley Press, 1997), 109-13.

18. This point is made by Rohrbaugh, *Biblical Interpreter*, 84. The sermons by Brueggemann and Taylor, cited in n. 17 above, manage to suggest the systemic complexities without resorting to didactic heavy-handedness.

7. Someone Sowed Good Seed

1. Bernard Brandon Scott, *Hear Then the Parable* (Minneapolis: Fortress Press, 1989), 68-70.

2. Robert W. Funk, Bernard Brandon Scott, and James R. Butts, *The Parables of Jesus: Red Letter Edition, A Report of the Jesus Seminar* (Sonoma, Calif.: Polebridge Press, 1982), 65.

3. Scott, *Hear Then the Parable*, 70.

4. Joachim Jeremias proposed that Jesus offered the parable to the Pharisees; *The Parables of Jesus* (trans. S. H. Hooke; 2nd rev. ed.; New York: Charles Scribner's Sons, 1972), 223-24. John R. Donahue concurs; *The Gospel in Parable* (Philadelphia: Fortress Press, 1988), 67.

5. Arland J. Hultgren suggests that the parable could have been addressed to disciples concerned about the company Jesus kept; *The Parables of Jesus: A Commentary* (Grand Rapids: Eerdmans, 2000), 300.

6. Opinion is mixed on whether Thomas is dependent on the Synoptics. Hultgren, for instance, maintains that Thomas draws from Matthew for the parable of the weeds (*Parables of Jesus*, 295). But a growing body of scholarship points to the independence of Thomas; see Charles W. Hedrick, *Parables as Poetic Fictions: The Creative Voice of Jesus* (Peabody, Mass.: Hendrickson, 1994), 249-51. Though some argue that both Matthew and Thomas drew from an early Christian invention (so Scott), the two sources may well represent dual attestation to an authentic Jesus tradition.

7. Fragments of a core parable of Jesus are located in 13:24b, 26, 28b-29 by Eduard Schweizer, *The Good News according to Matthew* (trans. David E. Green; Atlanta: John Knox Press, 1975), 303. Jack Dean Kingsbury attributes 13:24b-26 to Jesus; *The Parables of Jesus in Matthew 13: A Study in Redaction Criticism* (Richmond: John Knox Press, 1969), 65.

8. See Kingsbury, *Parables of Jesus*, 130-37.

9. Jeremias, *Parables of Jesus*, 82-84.

10. Douglas R. A. Hare states, "Perhaps Matthew was less pleased than Jesus with God's long-suffering!" *Matthew* (Interpretation; Louisville: John Knox Press, 1993), 155. It may be added that the *Gospel of Thomas*, while including the parable, reports no such interpretation of it.

11. That the parable is to be read independently of 13:36-43 is a matter of scholarly consensus. Hultgren puts it gently: "It is clear that there are major differences in meaning between the parable and the interpretation, and each must therefore be considered separately" (*Parables of Jesus*, 299). C. H. Dodd was less diplomatic: "We should do well to forget this interpretation as quickly as possible"; *The Parables of the Kingdom* (rev. ed.; New York: Charles Scribner's Sons, 1961), 148.

12. Eugene Boring, "The Gospel of Matthew" (vol. 8 of *The New Interpreter's Bible*; Nashville: Abingdon, 1995), 308.

13. Jeremias, *Parables of Jesus*, 225; see also Schweizer, *Good News*, 304.

14. Jeremias, *Parables of Jesus*, 224-25.

15. Hultgren, *Parables of Jesus*, 296.

16. John Dominic Crossan, *In Parables: The Challenge of the Historical Jesus* (New York: Harper & Row, 1973) 85; Donahue, *Gospel in Parable*, 67.

17. This is the final image of a sermon on the parable by Barbara Brown Taylor, *The Seeds of Heaven* (Cincinnati: Forward Movement Press, 1990), 19-20.

18. The painting, *The Harvest Is the End of the World and the Reapers Are Angels* (1984), is shown and discussed in Rupert Martin, "Roger Wagner's Visionary Landscapes," *Image* 10 (Summer 1995): 28-38.

19. Vivid examples are given in sermons by David Buttrick, *Speaking Parables: A Homiletic Guide* (Louisville: Westminster John Knox Press, 2000), 95-98; Barbara Brown Taylor, *Bread of Angels* (Cambridge, Mass.: Cowley Press, 1997), 146-50; Taylor, *Seeds of Heaven*, 15-20; Fred B. Craddock, *The Cherry Log Sermons* (Louisville: Westminster John Knox Press, 2001), 25-30; and Reinhold Niebuhr, *Justice and Mercy* (ed. Ursula M. Niebuhr; San Francisco: Harper & Row, 1974), 51-60.

8. A Rich Man Had a Manager

1. C. H. Dodd, *The Parables of the Kingdom* (rev. ed.; New York: Charles Scribner's Sons, 1961), 18; Joachim Jeremias, *The Parables of Jesus* (trans. S. H. Hooke; 2nd rev. ed.; New York: Charles Scribner's Sons, 1972), 45; John Dominic Crossan, *In Parables: The Challenge of the Historical Jesus* (New York: Harper & Row, 1973), 109.

2. Dodd famously imagined these verses as "notes for three separate sermons" (*Parables of the Kingdom*, 17). Kenneth Bailey argues that vv. 9-13 are a unified poem on mammon, likely spoken by Jesus, though not in connection with the parable, and placed here fittingly by Luke; *Poet and Peasant* (Grand Rapids: Eerdmans, 1976), 110-18.

3. The connection has been seen by many interpreters, among them T. H. Manson, *The Sayings of Jesus* (London: SCM Press, 1949), 291; Bailey, *Poet and Peasant*, 109; and most fruitfully by John R. Donahue, who lists ten parallels between the two stories and concludes that in light of them the parable of the

unjust steward might better be called the parable of the foolish master; *The Gospel in Parable* (Philadelphia: Fortress Press, 1988), 167-68.

4. This possibility is allowed by Jeremias, *Parables of Jesus*, 181, and by William R. Herzog II, *Parables as Subversive Speech: Jesus as Pedagogue of the Oppressed* (Louisville: Westminster/John Knox Press, 1994), 249-51.

5. J. D. Derrett, "Fresh Light on St. Luke XVI:1: Parable of the Unjust Steward," *New Testament Studies* 7 (1961): 198-219.

6. Jeremias, *Parables of Jesus*, 181.

7. Bernard Brandon Scott, *Hear Then the Parable* (Minneapolis: Fortress Press, 1989), 262, 265-66.

8. Herzog, *Parables as Subversive Speech*, 257.

9. Proponents of these views are, respectively, (1) Derrett, "Fresh Light," 198-219; Herzog, *Parables as Subversive Speech*, 255-57; (2) Joseph A. Fitzmyer, "The Story of the Dishonest Manager (Luke 16:1-13)," *Theological Studies* 25 (1964): 34-35; (3) Bailey, *Poet and Peasant*, 86-102; R. Alan Culpepper, "The Gospel of Luke" (vol. 9 of *The New Interpreter's Bible*; Nashville: Abingdon, 1995), 308; (4) Scott, *Hear Then the Parable*, 263-66; and (5) David Landry and Ben May, "Honor Restored: New Light on the Parable of the Unjust Steward (Luke 16:1-8a)," *Journal of Biblical Literature* 119 (2000): 287-309.

10. Proponents of these views are, respectively, (1) Luke 16:9; I. Howard Marshall, *Commentary on Luke* (New Testament Critical Commentary; Grand Rapids: Eerdmans, 1978), 622; Fred B. Craddock, *Luke* (Interpretation; Louisville: John Knox Press, 1990), 190-92; Francis Williams, "Is Almsgiving the Point of the 'Unjust Steward'?" *Journal of Biblical Literature* 83 (1964): 293-97; (2) Dodd, *Parables of the Kingdom*, 18; Jeremias, *Parables of Jesus*, 182; Bailey, *Poet and Peasant*, 117; (3) Dan Otto Via Jr., *The Parables: Their Literary and Existential Dimension* (Philadelphia: Fortress Press, 1967), 159-62; (4) Scott, *Hear Then the Parable*, 265; (5) Herzog, *Parables as Subversive Speech*, 258; (6) William Loader, "Jesus and the Rogue in Luke 16,1-8a: The Parable of the Unjust Steward," *Revue biblique* 96 (1989): 518-32; Robert Farrar Capon, *The Parables of Grace* (Grand Rapids: Eerdmans, 1988), 145-51; and (7) Paul Trudinger, "Exposing the Depths of Oppression (Luke 16:1b-8a)," in *Jesus and His Parables: Interpreting the Parables of Jesus Today* (ed. V. George Shillington; Edinburgh: T&T Clark, 1997), 121-37.

11. Herzog, *Parables as Subversive Speech*, 243-44, 252-53.

12. Herzog's description of the steward's plight, which I follow here, is persuasive (*Parables as Subversive Speech*, 241-42).

13. Bailey gives a fine account of the master's bind, caught between financial loss and celebrations in the village praising his generosity (*Poet and Peasant*, 101-2).

14. David Buttrick, *Speaking Parables: A Homiletic Guide* (Louisville: Westminster John Knox Press, 2000), 211.

15. I must credit Fred Craddock here. What I know of this method I learned by hearing him.

9. A Man Had Two Sons

1. John R. Donahue, *The Gospel in Parable* (Philadelphia: Fortress Press, 1988), 158.

2. J. D. Derrett, *Law in the New Testament* (London: Darton, Longman, and Todd, 1970), 105; Dan Otto Via Jr., *The Parables: Their Literary and Existential Dimension* (Philadelphia: Fortress Press, 1967), 169; Kenneth Bailey, *Poet and Peasant* (Grand Rapids: Eerdmans, 1976), 161; Bernard Brandon Scott, *Hear Then the Parable* (Minneapolis: Fortress Press, 1989), 111.

3. Joachim Jeremias, *The Parables of Jesus* (trans. S. H. Hooke; 2nd rev. ed.; New York: Charles Scribner's Sons, 1972), 129; Joseph A. Fitzmyer, *The Gospel according to Luke (X-XXIV)* (vol. 28A of *The Anchor Bible*; Garden City, N.Y.: Doubleday, 1985), 1086; Donahue, *Gospel in Parable*, 153.

4. Arland J. Hultgren, *The Parables of Jesus: A Commentary* (Grand Rapids: Eerdmans, 2000), 71.

5. In Eph 5:18 the word describes drunkenness; Titus 1:6 likens it to rebelliousness; in 1 Pet 4:3-4 it is a summary word for Gentile "excesses" like "licentiousness, passions, drunkenness, revels, carousing, and lawless idolatry."

6. Brad H.Young, *The Parables: Jewish Tradition and Christian Interpretation* (Peabody, Mass.: Hendrickson, 1998), 145; Scott, *Hear Then the Parable*, 115.

7. Those who present the prodigal as fully repentant include Jeremias, *Parables of Jesus*, 130; I. Howard Marshall, *Commentary on Luke* (New Testament Critical Commentary; Grand Rapids: Eerdmans, 1978), 607; and R. Alan Culpepper, "The Gospel of Luke" (vol. 9 of *The New Interpreter's Bible*; Nashville: Abingdon, 1995), 302; those who suggest otherwise include Bailey, *Poet and Peasant*, 173-75; Donahue, *Gospel in Parable*, 153; Scott, *Hear Then the Parable*, 115-16; Hultgren, *Parables of Jesus*, 76.

8. Hultgren, *Parables of Jesus*, 76-77.

9. Jeremias, *Parables of Jesus*, 130; Bailey, *Poet and Peasant*, 181; Donahue, *Gospel in Parable*, 155. Scott says the father's response has "the quality of burlesque" (*Hear Then the Parable*, 117).

10. Bailey, *Poet and Peasant*, 181; Richard L. Rohrbaugh, "A Dysfunctional Family and Its Neighbors," in *Jesus and His Parables: Interpreting the Parables of Jesus Today* (ed. V. George Shillington; Edinburgh: T&T Clark, 1997), 156. A fine sermonic account of the father running the gauntlet of hostile villagers for his son is given by H. Stephen Shoemaker, *Godstories: New Narratives from Sacred Texts* (Valley Forge: Judson Press, 1998), 246-47.

11. Bailey, *Peasant and Poet*, 195; Scott, *Hear Then the Parable*, 120; Rohrbaugh, "Dysfunctional Family," 159-60.

12. The consistently "maternal" behaviors of this father have inspired rich reflection. Henri Nouwen notes that Rembrandt's painting of the parable seems to depict one of the father's hands as masculine and the other as feminine; *The Return of the Prodigal: A Story of Homecoming* (New York: Doubleday, 1992), 99. Sandra Schneiders writes: "Jesus' parable about the father actually constitutes a radical challenge to patriarchy. The divine father who has been understood as the ultimate justification of human patriarchy is revealed as the one who refuses to own us, demand our submission or punish our rebellion. Rather, God is the one who respects our freedom, mourns our alienation, waits patiently for our return and accepts our love as pure gift." *Women and the Word: The Gender of God in the New Testament and the Spirituality of Women* (1986 Madeleva Lecture in Spirituality; Mahwah, N.J.: Paulist, 1986). Quoted by Donahue, *Gospel in Parable*, 161-62.

13. Peter Rhea Jones draws attention to this motif; *Studying the Parables of Jesus* (Macon, Ga.: Smyth & Helwys, 1999), 227-28.

14. This is Scott's language, *Hear Then the Parable*, 121.

15. Ibid., 123-25. Scott has argued that the parable assaults Israel's "mytheme" of being the younger son (Jacob) favored at the expense of others.

16. See Mikeal C. Parsons, "The Prodigal's Elder Brother: The History and Ethics of Reading Luke 15:25-32," *Perspectives in Religious Studies* 23 (Summer 1966): 147-74.

17. L. Susan Bond has argued that the preaching of all parables, at least to socially privileged congregations, must work strictly from a single point of view, that of the parables' privileged characters, whose status is always subverted; "Taming the Parables: The Problem of Parable as Sabotage Myth," *Homiletic* 25, no. 1 (Summer 2000): 1-12. This parable in my view constitutes a resounding exception. Nouwen, cited above, offers useful identifications with both sons (and an invitation to identify even with the father).

10. On Preaching Parables

1. Leander E. Keck, *The Bible in the Pulpit: The Renewal of Biblical Preaching* (Nashville: Abingdon, 1978), 142. Others have made similar confessions. John Dominic Crossan wrote in a preface to a book on the parables: "One wonders what the maker of parables must think of the maker of comments. What would the parabolic mind say to the exegetical mind if, just for once, it had the chance?" *In Parables: The Challenge of the Historical Jesus* (New York: Harper & Row, 1973), xv-xvi.

2. Paul Ricoeur, "The Bible and the Imagination," in *The Bible as Document of the University* (ed. H. D. Betz; Chico, Calif.: Scholars Press, 1981), 81.

3. Fred B. Craddock, *The Gospels* (Interpreting Biblical Texts; Nashville: Abingdon, 1981), 113.

4. C. H. Dodd, *The Parables of the Kingdom* (rev. ed.; New York: Charles Scribner's Sons, 1961), 5.

5. See pp. 72, 74-75.

6. For more on this, see David Buttrick, *Speaking Parables: A Homiletic Guide* (Louisville: Westminster John Knox Press, 2000), 51-52.

7. John Dominic Crossan, *The Dark Interval: Towards a Theology of Story* (Sonoma, Calif.: Polebridge, 1988), 121.

8. Some interpreters claim that all parables do the same thing and that words ascribed to Jesus that do not conform cannot be among his parables. Such reductionism is to be rejected. Thomas G.Long argues at length that preachers must recognize differences in parable type and function; *Preaching and the Literary Forms of the Bible* (Philadelphia: Fortress, 1989), 87-106.

9. For examples, see p. 10.

10. See pp. 9-10, 70.

11. See Fernando Segovia and Mary Ann Tolbert, *Reading from This Place: Social Location and Biblical Interpretation in Global Perspective* (Minneapolis: Fortress, 1995).

12. Such help can be found in the works we have cited by Kenneth Bailey, William R. Herzog II, Richard L. Rohrbaugh, and others who read the parables from a social-science perspective.

13. William R. Herzog II suggests that Jesus told many of his parables "for the purpose of generating conversation," particularly about justice; *Parables as Subversive Speech: Jesus as Pedagogue of the Oppressed* (Louisville: Westminster/John Knox Press, 1994), 26. Crossan concurs: "The function of Jesus' parables about the kingdom of God was to create debate about justice. . . . They lured the audience into self-education." John Dominic Crossan, "The Parables of Jesus," *Interpretation* 56 (July 2002): 253.

14. Richard Lischer, "The Limits of Story," *Interpretation* 38, no. 1 (January 1984): 27.

15. See pp. 50-56.

16. R. Alan Culpepper, "Parable as Commentary: The Twice-Given Vineyard," *Perspectives in Religious Studies* 26 (Summer 1999): 147-68.

17. Buttrick, *Speaking Parables*, 41. Along with the verse-by-verse approach, he rejects topical and "life-situation" sermons on the parables; 39-40. I do not address the latter two options, having already argued that the parable as parable should shape and control the sermon.

18. For examples, see Buttrick, *Speaking Parables*, 49-51.

19. See pp. 27-28, 34-36, 40-41, 54-55, 65, 95-96.

20. Heard in a sermon by the incomparable Grady Nutt.

21. The sermon was published in H. Stephen Shoemaker, *Retelling the Biblical Story: The Theology and Practice of Narrative Preaching* (Nashville: Broadman, 1985), 126-32. He discusses the strategy of anachronism on p. 169.

22. Sallie McFague, *Metaphorical Theology: Models of God in Religious Language* (Philadelphia: Fortress Press, 1982), 42-43.

23. Arland J. Hultgren, *The Parables of Jesus: A Commentary* (Grand Rapids: Eerdmans, 2000), 1.

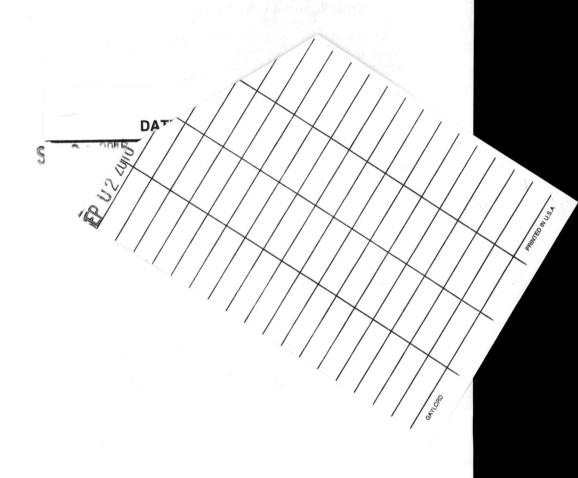